Paul and Paula

Paul and Paula

A Story of Separation, Survival and Belonging

Tim McNamara

Published by Monash University Publishing
Matheson Library Annexe
40 Exhibition Walk
Monash University
Clayton, Victoria 3800, Australia
publishing.monash.edu

Monash University Publishing: the discussion starts here

Tim McNamara © Copyright 2023
Tim McNamara reserves the right to be known as the author of this work.

All rights reserved. Apart from any uses permitted by Australia's *Copyright Act 1968*, no part of this book may be reproduced by any process without prior written permission from the copyright owners. Enquiries should be directed to the publisher.

Reasonable attempts have been made to locate copyright holders, and any potential infringement of copyright is accidental. Should any infringement be suspected, contact Monash University Publishing.

Paul and Paula: A Story of Separation, Survival and Belonging

ISBN: 9781922979377 (paperback)
ISBN: 9781922979384 (PDF)
ISBN: 9781922979391 (ePub)

Cover design by Leslie Thomas
Typesetting by Joanne Mullins

Quote on p.17 reproduced with kind permission from Di Cowan

 A catalogue record for this book is available from the National Library of Australia

Printed in Australia by Griffin Press

Contents

Preface vii

PART 1: GENERATIONS 1

Chapter 1   Fathers 3

Chapter 2   Vienna 29

Chapter 3   Paul 64

PART 2: PAUL AND PAULA 83

Chapter 1   Leaving Vienna
             April 1939 87

Chapter 2   The Build-up to War
             April to August 1939 98

Chapter 3   The Outbreak of War
             September 1939 to May 1940 105

Chapter 4   Internment and Deportation
             May to July 1940 119

Chapter 5   *Dunera*
             July to September 1940 128

Chapter 6	Vienna	
	July to November 1940	133
Chapter 7	Hay	
	September 1940 to May 1941	138
Chapter 8	Vienna	
	November 1940 to June 1941	143
Chapter 9	Vienna: The Last Letters	
	June to December 1941	153
Chapter 10	Tatura; Melbourne	
	May 1941 to May 1943; 1943 to 1945	158
Chapter 11	Vienna: After the Letters Stopped	
	January 1942 to early 1943	166
Chapter 12	Vienna; Melbourne	
	1945 to 1947	176
Chapter 13	Coda	185

Postscript, 2021 193
Acknowledgements 197
About the Author 199

Preface

Paul Kurz, a Jewish refugee from Vienna, a Dunera Boy, interned in Australia, wrote to his brother-in-law from an internment camp in Australia in 1942: 'But never mind, in fifty years it's all the same and nobody will then know anything about our troubles.' As he waited in internment without definitive news of the fate of his wife, Paula, trapped in Vienna, where the remaining 68,000 Jews were being sent systematically to their deaths, he wrote: 'It is now more than one year I last heard from her, and that is not very easy to bear. But in fifty years' time, it is all the same.'

Eighty years after he wrote those words, the story of Paul's 'troubles' is told here. It is based on his own words, and those of his wife and her family in Vienna, in letters sent to his brother-in-law Walter in New York. My friend Pat, Walter's daughter, found and translated the letters after her father's death and shared them with me. The letters form the basis of Paul and Paula's story in the second part of this book.

The first part, however, is about my relationship with Paul. I met Paul when I was twenty and he was close to seventy. Our connection was made across a generational span and vast differences of culture and history: me, a naive young Australian from a tortured Catholic background; him, marked by the violence of the Holocaust. Thirty years after Paul's death, I explored his hometown, Vienna, the city he had wanted to show me while he was still alive. Gradually, its history, its beauty, its violence, its cruelty, what he loved and what he suffered there revealed itself to me.

This book is in part a biography of Paul and his painful separation from Paula, and also a story of my bond with Paul and the impact he had on my life. He strongly believed in the randomness and inescapability of fate, a fate which was often unbearably cruel. But fate in my case was kind, connecting me to Paul, and to his wisdom. Now older than Paul was when I met him, I am nurtured to this day by his felt presence. This is his story, and ours.

Part 1
Generations

Chapter 1

Fathers

Those evenings at 'Uncle Paul's' place I remember vividly, though they were more than fifty years ago. The evenings started in 1968. I was nineteen, a fellow literature student and one of the university friends of Pat, the American niece of Paul's late wife, Paula. Paul was a widower, with no children. Pat had come to Melbourne from New York on exchange for a year, though the year ultimately extended into three. Paul was two generations older than us, old enough to be our grandfather, not tall, wore a beret indoors – extraordinary to my provincial eyes – and spoke English fluently, with a German accent. He was warm, generous, critical, welcoming, courteous. He engaged with us, took us seriously, wanted to educate us. Paul was a Jewish refugee from Vienna. The Holocaust was in the background but never mentioned or discussed explicitly; our conversations were all about Pat and me, our youth, and our future. I was drawn to the richness and intelligence of Paul's world. It was so utterly different to mine.

Paul lived in a beautiful, modernist house. In 1953 he had commissioned a young architect, Alistair Knox, still in the first stage of his career, to design a house for him in what was then a new suburb in the east of Melbourne, about 10 kilometres from the central business district. The work of Knox at that time showed the influence of Frank Lloyd Wright and his pupil Walter Burley Griffin, the designer of Canberra. As Richard Peterson and Bohdan Kuzyk wrote in the *RMIT Design Archives Journal*, 'Knox's approach was modernist in its embrace of light, space, proportion, unadorned minimalism, modularity and orientation. His buildings sit empathetically within the natural landscape.' The house was on a sloping block, with a garage and workshop on the lower floor, and the main part of the house built above it. From the street, the house appeared to be single storey, with a flat roof, and painted a quiet grey. The garden was planted with native trees, including a lemon-scented gum, which suited it perfectly (Knox was also known as a landscape architect), though the style of the house and the garden were strikingly different from the bland new brick-veneer houses and European gardens that filled this and the neighbouring streets. I realised years later that Paul was bringing to Melbourne a taste for the kind of modernist aesthetic in architecture that was distinctive of Vienna.

Inside, the living room had a parquet floor with Oriental rugs, richly filled bookshelves, a sofa and chairs, and on small tables next to the armchair were books that Paul was reading – Joyce's *Ulysses*, in English, was one. The room was rather dark; the drapes were kept drawn. In one corner was a round dining room table and chairs, with a servery from the kitchen behind the table. There was an overhead light on a cord above the table, with a burgundy-coloured wicker shade, creating an intimate space for conversation. Paul would make dinner for us – Pat and her friends, all of us studying literature together. Typically it was fillet steak, boiled potatoes and wonderfully new things – *Kaisersemmeln* (Kaiser rolls, the dough enfolded in a characteristic way) that were, as I subsequently discovered, typical of Vienna; a cordial drink with lemonade and raspberry syrup that we continued to make and called the 'Valmai drink', after our friend Valmai who was part of the student circle; and *Gurkensalat* (cucumber salad) which Paul taught me to make one evening. You cut the peeled cucumbers extremely finely, then sprinkled them slightly with salt; after a while you squeezed the slices against the ball of the hand to drain off the bitter juice. They were then marinated in slightly sweetened lemon juice and water, topped with some very fine slices of onion, and seasoned. Decades later, I recognised this dish in a *heuriger*, a vineyard tavern in the hills around Vienna.

Our conversations under the dinner table light were always intense – we were deeply engaged in our literature studies, and it was a time of great political and cultural change, triggered by the events in the United States, and the Vietnam War, in which Australia was a participant. There was conscription of eighteen-year-olds (I had been called up but had got a deferment until the end of my studies). Paul commented gently on our discovery of personal and sexual freedoms in this new cultural environment, a pale shadow of the anarchic freedoms of Vienna in his youth. One of the books on his shelves was about Chagall. He saw me looking through it one evening. As an intense but troubled Catholic, I was moved and intrigued to see images Chagall had painted during the Holocaust of the crucified Christ as an Orthodox Jewish man with a prayer shawl. 'You believe we killed God,' Paul said. The comment provoked me terribly, and I couldn't stop thinking about it. It took me years to understand it, and to finally accept its truth. Another image was a portrait of Chagall's first wife, Bella, who had died suddenly in 1944. I could see that the painting, full of love for its subject, had a special significance for Paul, that it connected to his grief over Paula.

Paul and Paula

What sort of person was I when I met Paul? Why was I so drawn to his warmth and care for me, as well his sadness, his tragic experience?

*

My father's sixtieth birthday was 4 June 1973, the day of his retirement after more than forty years in the bank for which he worked. The retirement was relatively early, at sixty, and probably not of his choosing. A party at home had been organised for the Saturday night to mark the birthday and retirement. It was a big month: I was leaving indefinitely for Europe, my first time overseas, on 23 June with my friend Lillian. I was twenty-four, and the date of the party was my last chance to have dinner at Paul's place before I left. So, I told my parents that I would not be there. This elicited an angry response in my father, which was unusual, as he was well-liked for his easy-going manner, and the anger in his words had a violent, unrestrained edge. My mother was furious too, but it was my father who took the lead on this occasion. I stood my ground – or rather slunk into my burrow, full of a corresponding anger, not easily expressed, but which had a cold, resentful intensity.

How had we got to this point? Why this betrayal of my father?

*

An early memory: I'm four, and it's after dinner in our rented postwar house in the raw new outer Melbourne suburb of Noble Park, the gas fire warming the living room, time for the family to say the rosary ('The family that prays together, stays together'). I go down on my knees, propping myself up against the small elegant 'ladies' chair' with its curved rosewood back; my father kneels against the larger companion armchair, and my mother, older sister and brother against the lounge suite. The murmured antiphonal prayers go on, Dad leading, 'Second Sorrowful Mystery: The Scourging at the Pillar. Hail Mary, full of grace, the Lord is with thee, blessèd art thou among women, and blessèd is the fruit of thy womb, Jesus', the rest of the family chorusing in response: 'Holy Mary, Mother of God, pray for us sinners now and at the hour of our death. Amen.' And again, ten times, the smooth black wooden rosary beads slipping between the fingers, until they feel a longer chain link and a larger bead indicating that the decade is over. And then the next of the five Sorrowful Mysteries, The Crowning with Thorns, (on other days of the week the Glorious Mysteries, or the Joyful Mysteries); five decades in all, one for each mystery.

I pretend to fall asleep before the end of the Hail Marys, and remain motionless, eyes closed, when we reach the final prayer. The deception works: Dad comes and picks me up. I love the feeling as he carries me to my bed in the adjoining room, a formal dining room but used as a bedroom for me and my older brother, the light from the living room visible through the bubbled-glass partition doors. I'm sound asleep before it is time for my parents to turn in under the watchful eye of the image of the Sacred Heart of Jesus above their bed. This is the first of only two times in my childhood that Dad holds me or hugs me – my brother remembers three times in his. The second is in the backyard, still at Noble Park, on a frosty night, as we all stand around looking up at the dark sky, and Dad points out the rings around the moon; perhaps there was some phenomenon like a comet that we were meant to see as well.

It's Saturday, and I must be five, still at Noble Park. Dad and I are in the backyard, working a garden bed just next to the kitchen steps. Much excitement: Mum is off to the races, a special occasion, and is dressed up and about to leave. It must be the Caulfield Cup, one of the two big races of the Spring Racing Carnival. The racetrack at Caulfield is a long suburban train ride away, but an easier destination than the more famous track at Flemington where the Melbourne Cup is run, far away in a suburb on the other side of the city. She opens the flywire screen on the back door from the kitchen and stands on the concrete step to say goodbye – I look up: skirt, stockings, shoes, at eye level. It's okay for her to go; I'm going to spend the afternoon with Dad, digging, planting vegetables. His bible is a much-loved Yates *Garden Guide*, dog-eared, torn, dusty with blood and bone; and he is following the golden rule, planting his tomato seedlings and sowing the beans between Caulfield Cup Day and Melbourne Cup Day.

When we move to our own house in Essendon the following year, I get my own small garden bed under the apple tree in the backyard, where I grow radishes and carrots. Dad is tall and slim, good-looking in those days, wiry and strong, with black hair, an Aussie country lad all his life. He has impressive beds of tomatoes, and French beans and broad beans sown in neat, built-up rows. Nearby, a vast compost heap and piles of firewood. A passionfruit vine made prolific by the rich material from Mr Stone's chook run next door separates this area from the main backyard area closer to the house, large and empty, suitable for footy and cricket against the wooden door of the fibro garage. I am hopeless at both, and not keen to play, to the annoyance of the other males in my family, though I am a keen fan of the footy team the family supports, St Kilda, the Saints. The bowler at cricket has to bowl around a large, abundant plum tree; after some years

Dad chops it down to make a straighter pitch. Without the tree the backyard looks even bleaker, a tall, grey, wooden paling fence separates us from the Stones next door, the back view with the horizontal timber struts, good for climbing, on our side; occasional shrubs struggle in the garden beds, hydrangeas, a weigela, some irises.

My best friend and I are inseparable, twelve, on the cusp of puberty. We climb up the back fence on my side and into the peach tree, me ahead, when I feel his hand groping me from behind. I say nothing, shrug him off. Another day, we are playing with his meccano set in his bedroom, and he grabs me from behind again. I say nothing, shrug him off. I'm not sure what it's about, but I know it's 'dirty', and therefore wrong. It happens a third time, as we clean bricks for a penny a brick in a neighbour's garage – and that's it, the friendship is abruptly ended. I say nothing to my parents. My mother notices that I'm no longer playing with him and asks me about it, but I make some non-committal reply and it's not mentioned again. Dad doesn't seem to notice; it's not something I could tell him about.

It must have hurt my friend a lot, but that was something I realised only much later, after I had acknowledged my own sexuality.

*

It's hard to convey the intense boundedness of the world in which I grew up. It was exclusively Irish Catholic. Even Uncle Ken, and mum's best friend, Molly, who had become Catholics in order to marry their spouses, were referred to as 'converts': they were welcomed, and loved, but marked. Our house was close to St Teresa's church and primary school, just at the end of our block. Our neighbours on one side were the Misses Looby, three Irish sisters, Catholic, unmarried, 'old maids' as we used to say, probably in their sixties and seventies. While we were on good terms with our other neighbours, the Stones, they, being Presbyterian, were kept at a certain distance. Even though Italian, Maltese, Yugoslav and Polish migrants – Pribaz, Bertoncello, Zuliani, Boffa, Jakoljovic, Rossi, Caruana – were an ever more visible presence in our church community and in our classes at school, they were never part of the family friendship group. My cousin Sally married an Australian-born Italian, Salvatore, and my aunt, Sally's mother, though a warm, generous and immensely good-humoured person, never allowed anyone to forget that Salvatore's family was different. So, although we saw ourselves as thoroughly Australian, traditional Irish Catholic attitudes and values had been passed on in an unbroken line in this Australian environment in an encapsulated community over the 120 years since my father's ancestor had arrived three years after the establishment of the original colonial settlement in Melbourne: his address was 'Canvas Town, Bourke Street, Melbourne'. Our education was conducted separately: it was a mortal sin for parents not to send their children to the Catholic parochial schools, as the priest regularly reminded the congregation at the obligatory Sunday Mass.

Although religious affiliation thus bound us tightly, the tone of religious piety was leavened in an Australian, or perhaps Irish, way. On the day of Dad's funeral, my sister told me a story he had told her. Later in life, with the children grown up and gone, he and my mother slept in individual beds, in the same bedroom. My mother insisted that they say the rosary together as they lay in bed. My father discovered that if he said his response in the Hail Marys in a sing-song voice, he could make my mother fall asleep faster: his goal was to get her to fall asleep by the end of the first decade. My mother and her very pious, alcoholic sister-in-law would say the rosary together in the late afternoon, and then have a sherry. I commented once that it was right that they said the rosary first, and then had the sherry. 'Oh no, dear,' my mother answered, 'we have a sherry, and then we say the rosary, and then we have another sherry.'

While Dad was committed to his role as a father to his four growing children – taking us on picnics and trips to the beach, and to the footy, acknowledging our day over dinner – there was nevertheless a sense of absence. Each day, he would spend an hour at the pub, taking part in the 'six o'clock swill', the period of feverish drinking after work and before the pubs closed at 6 pm, as part of the restrictive licensing hours. He would arrive home with a further two large bottles of beer in a brown paper bag under his arm. During the evening after dinner, he would sit quietly in the big rosewood chair and make his way through the two bottles, smoking and reading the evening broadsheet, *The Herald*.

The fact that Dad drank beer, and lots of it, was unremarkable in our hard-drinking culture. He was born in the country, in northern Victoria; his father had worked in the family firm of stock and station agents, well known throughout the area. His father had died when Dad was in his early teens, and Dad never really fit in with the middle-class aspirations and expectations of the women (my grandmother and his three sisters) who raised and somewhat spoiled him, no doubt a reminder of their loss. The family's investments were wiped out in the Depression; they moved to Melbourne, where my father got a job in the bank, based on his copperplate handwriting, in an extremely tough job market. He never fitted into the bank, with its conservative ethos and its expectations of the social role required of its staff, particularly its branch managers. The pay was relatively poor, the attraction of the position being its social status, but this never mattered to my father;

in fact it, was something of a handicap. My mother came from a banking family from the same rural area; Dad's mother and Mum's mother knew each other, which is how my parents met. My father learnt to play the roles required of him but never took the reins in the marriage. His lack of confidence was perhaps the reason for his drinking, which was the quiet, steady type, just beer, no spirits, and never any scenes or violence. It was a habit he no doubt acquired as a young single man living in a boarding house in St Kilda until his marriage at twenty-seven, and then his five years in the army during the war. The empty beer bottles stacked at the side of the house, out of the way, steadily accumulated. Bottle-os would come by from time to time, in horse-drawn carts, calling out 'Bottle-o' as they went past, and would stop and pay a penny a bottle, or was it a penny a dozen bottles, which, either way, given the prodigious number of bottles we had, amounted to a tidy sum. My father would let us have the money from the bottle-o, so we never minded how many empty bottles there were; it created a positive association with my father's drinking.

In our Australian Irish Catholic culture, everybody drank, and non-drinkers – known disparagingly as 'wowsers', 'teetotallers' – stood out, thought of as not being good fun. As a boy I never thought there was a problem with this; it seemed so normal. A brother and a sister of my mother were, unlike my father, rather obvious alcoholics, as was another aunt by marriage. My uncle on the other hand, my father's best friend, was a prodigious drinker too, but seemed unaffected by it and was able to give up easily. He used to greet my father with the nickname 'shicker', Australian slang for drunk (ironically a word from Yiddish originally): 'G'day, shick', he'd cheerfully say as he arrived for a pre-dinner beer with my father (my mother and his wife had sherries). But by the time my father was fifty, things had got out of control.

While the true story of what happened took many years to emerge, and remains somewhat unclear, it seems that my father's drinking had finally got the better of him.

He had by now been promoted to the position of bank manager. My father was a most unlikely bank manager: he was not a reserved middle-class man; instead, people thought of him as the stereotypical Australian, with a broad accent, a colourful use of Australian slang, a friendly manner with clients and a kind of easy-going optimism. His three appointments to managerial positions were all in suburbs with high migrant densities: first in the brand-new outer-northwestern suburb of Merlynston, then in inner-city Brunswick and North Fitzroy. He prided himself on the loans he made to enterprising migrants who needed someone to trust their energy and determination, rather than demanding proof of their non-existent capital. Though my father's professional relationships with his migrant clients were supportive and cordial – he believed in a 'fair go' for people – the migrants themselves remained fundamentally 'other'.

However, instead of being out visiting clients, apparently my father would be at the pub shortly after it opened at 11 am. Initially his accountant, with the loyalty of that generation that had served in the war together, covered for him. But the bank finally got wind of what was going on and he was immediately relieved of his managerial position. He didn't disclose the real reason to my mother, who indignantly insisted on a meeting with the general manager of the bank at the head office in Collins Street in the centre of Melbourne, at which she would accompany my father and demand an explanation. The appointment was made, and only as they were sitting outside the manager's office waiting to be called in did my father finally blurt out what had been going on. My mother was, of course, humiliated, and furious – she had a 'fine Irish temper', so the saying goes – but was determined not to show it, and to cover up for my father, as her pride mattered above all. He was then, cruelly, given the role of relieving manager at country branches, if the regular manager was ill or on leave. Cruel, because it involved long nights alone in country towns far from Melbourne; he would return home only on weekends. Finally, he was given a pen-pushing job at the head office – the bank didn't sack managers in those days, it would have caused a scandal – until the earliest possible date for his retirement, when he turned sixty.

I was fourteen as the crisis came to a head, and I was difficult, demanding, as adolescence and its confusing and troubling feelings began to emerge. A photo from the time shows me in school uniform with a prefect's badge, newly tall and ungainly, intensely self-conscious, enduring the photo-taking with clenched fists. I was increasingly curious and confident intellectually, doing exceptionally well at school – I was called a 'brain' – and took my religion very seriously. At the Catholic high school I was attending we had an hour of religious instruction every day, and annual school retreats where we were given intense spiritual training. The imaginative richness and complexity of the church rituals throughout the course of the year appealed to me intellectually and poetically. But the religious intensity had a deeper, problematic emotional basis. Guilt about sex had begun to dominate my consciousness and what was referred to as 'self-abuse'. I remember the first time I masturbated, when I was twelve or thirteen. From my darkened bedroom I could hear the noise of the television and see the light from the living room. I lay face down, rubbing myself against the sheets, and came messily. My immediate response was intense guilt: I didn't know what had happened, or what it meant, but I knew it was wrong – I had committed my first mortal sin. And the sin, always fought against, became an ongoing issue, never discussed with anyone – certainly not my schoolmates or my brothers – other than the priest in confession. Offences against God came in two sizes – mortal and venial. Mortal included things such as murder and masturbation. If you died in a state of mortal sin you would go straight to Hell. I would do anything to avoid committing such a sin, but I couldn't help myself. I tried attending Mass every weekday morning, whipping myself up into a kind of religious frenzy, and this would work, until I yielded momentarily to desire. My aunt, a nun, had given me a plaster statue of Jesus showing his bleeding Sacred Heart, and I would turn it to face the wall when the impulse to masturbate overcame me. The briefest of pleasures would be followed by intense guilt and an act of contrition, seeking God's forgiveness, which would mean I wouldn't go to Hell, just to Purgatory. But this act of contrition did not mean you were in a 'state of grace' and so able to receive Communion during Mass. You needed to go to confession for that. I confessed my sins, using the standard formula: 'I have been impure, in deed, by myself, twice.' A problem arose if I masturbated on a Saturday night, because there was no opportunity to confess the sin, as confessions were usually held on Saturday morning. This meant avoiding attending Mass with the family, because I would not be able to take Communion. Taking Communion when you were not in a state of grace was 'the sin against the Holy Ghost', the most terrible sin one could commit, worse than murder. I would have to get up early and go to the earliest Mass, before my parents were up and about, preparing to go to their Mass, attendance at which was obligatory in those days – failure to do so was another mortal sin. On one occasion I sought advice from the priest about what I could do to avoid this sin. 'Have you thought of tying rosary beads around your hand?'

'Oh, so that as I unwound them I would think of Our Lady and overcome the temptation?'

'No, just that it would hurt.'

I realise now looking back that I had no or hardly any sexual fantasies – my obsessive sexual activities, so preoccupied with resistance, momentary yielding, guilt and shame, never involved thoughts of other people, certainly not girls. The nearest thing to a sexual response to girls was when I was fourteen watching the opening number of the film *Bye Bye Birdie*, with the Swedish-born actress Ann-Margret in a tight low-cut yellow dress against a vivid-blue background, singing the title song. But even that was not a visceral feeling, more an intellectual discovery. My furtive feelings involved three boys – school and family friends – around that time. But I didn't understand these attractions and I was defensive against recognising their significance. I was totally naive when it came to sex and didn't understand the mechanics of it until I was about sixteen or seventeen.

Sexual desire was not the only feeling I suppressed. Another was a subconscious rage at my father, which revealed itself to me once, briefly, in a flash of feeling, which I was too shocked to understand or explore. In our English class we were reading short stories by Australian authors. Peter Cowan's 'The Red-Backed Spiders' was set in the physically and emotionally bleak farming country far from Perth in Western Australia. The boy in the story occupies himself by playing in the rubbish heap, building things using empty tins. His embittered, frustrated father warns him not to play there: it's dangerous, there are venomous red-backed spiders in the tins. The boy persists and makes his most creative structure yet – a castle, with turrets and walls – which is destroyed by the angry father when he sees it. At dusk that evening, an itinerant farmhand – the narrator – notices the boy carrying some empty tins towards the house. In the middle of the night there is a great commotion: the father is critically ill, apparently from spider bites, and is taken to hospital. No one inquires how this could have happened, and the matter is soon forgotten.

This story struck me like a bolt of lightning. I identified with the boy and this passage:

> The boy wanted his father, and his world was so plainly incomplete without him. He would still go up to his father to talk to him, sometimes for the affection that seemed now inevitably denied, that had perhaps never been there, sometimes to ask the questions that his mind was filled with and that were reduced quickly to the man's ridicule. So that he was become now too quiet and solitary for a boy of his age.

However, I was not quiet and solitary – the family group consciousness within which I was wholly formed didn't encourage private introspection – but I needed the love of my father, who, although he was very different from the man in the story, not obviously bitter or harshly critical, was increasingly consumed by his drinking and its disastrous consequences, and was absent emotionally.

Throughout my adolescence I remained religiously devout. But gradually, in my final year of high school and throughout my university years, it slowly all came undone. After four years of intense, almost daily, questioning of the existence of God, the linchpin of my entire world, explored through my literary and historical studies in my degree, and an accompanying sexual confusion, the dam abruptly burst, and in a terrifyingly public way, at the beginning of my Honours year. During what was to be a nationally televised debate on the topic

'Is the Catholic Church in Australia today reactionary?', in which I had volunteered to be the student representative arguing the opposing case, along with a nun and a priest, it all fell apart. In a single, dizzying moment, halfway through my presentation, I realised I no longer believed the increasingly tortured arguments I was making to justify the existence of God as the basis for defending the Church. A prominent, good-looking student from the floor had interrupted my presentation with a provocatively embarrassing question – 'So, if the Mass is just a meal, would you take your girlfriend to Mass, not to dinner?' I had no girlfriend, and worse, I realised that I was attracted to the student who had asked the question. The fragile edifice of my belief finally collapsed. I immediately back-pedalled, and the debate descended into confusion. Fortunately, I don't think the debate was ever broadcast. My father had driven me to the debate, to be a supportive presence there, and he was in the audience and witnessed my failure, my fall, but said nothing as we drove home. I'm not sure if he had understood what had happened.

The year had begun so badly with this public humiliation, the crucial final year of my degree, and it continued to worsen as the year went on: I was having a protracted and severe nervous breakdown. My mother was concerned, and tried to reach me as I withdrew into my anxiety, but we were not a family used to discussing difficult emotional issues – my father's drinking was the elephant in the room – and my obvious departure from the family values, sometimes sharply expressed, was provocative. One day during the course of the year, I confessed to my father my attraction to guys, but my confession was met with a punishing silence. His shoulders slumped, he left the room, and never spoke to me about it again, nor to my mother, it seemed.

Within a few months of intensifying emotional difficulties, I moved out of home (recommended, to my surprise and relief, by the family GP), got a loan from the university to pay my rent and buy food, experienced the onset of psychotic hallucinations, and collapsed during the final year examinations. I had a few sessions, all I could afford, with a psychiatrist, who prescribed a powerful, now banned, antipsychotic drug. I had increasing crushes on guys, failed a humiliating army medical, which I had to take now that I had completed my studies, and had embarrassing failures at successive job interviews. My present and future were increasingly frightening. The letter from the psychiatrist to the army stated that I had a 'guarded prognosis'. My friends withdrew in confusion: 'They flee from me that sometime did me seek', in the words of the poet Wyatt.

Only one person reacted differently, a fellow student in my literature class. Her name was Lillian. We had first connected the previous year during a discussion of *The Brothers Karamazov*, Dostoevsky's great novel of existential doubt. I had taken the novel very seriously, as it addressed precisely the questions that were preoccupying me. I read the novel as an affirmation of faith, and when invited to contribute to the discussion, formulated my response by saying the book made me 'glad I was a Catholic'. Lillian, who I had a sense admired me academically, gave me a dismissive look, and I realised that she, unlike the rest of the students in the class, had some insight into the significance of what I was saying. I ran after her in the corridor after the class had finished, explaining that what I had said was shorthand, that things were far less certain for me than my words had suggested, and that there was a lot to discuss. She listened, somewhat unconvinced. The following year, months into my breakdown, I gave a class paper on another book of Dostoevsky's, *Crime and Punishment,* and my perspective on his work had entirely changed, though the presentation was less clear, grasping, more confused. 'I actually prefer you like this,' she said, meaning the doubting, tortured soul she recognised, rather than the obnoxious Catholic ideologue of old. I knew little about her; a class discussion of George Eliot's *Daniel Deronda* had given a clue – when asked specifically by the lecturer to comment on the Jewish characters in the book, she replied that they were like Martians – entirely unreal and unconvincing. So, she was Jewish. Her answer displayed an intensity and originality; she was an anarchistic spirit in the class, known to be already living with her boyfriend and coming to class in a distinctive second-hand fur stole, not always having read what we were discussing, but capable of deep insights when called on to speak. Lillian was a vigorous atheist, a sexual libertarian and intensely political, and friends with those who were at the centre of political and cultural developments in the heady days of the student revolution, the sexual revolution, and the protests against the Vietnam War in the late 1960s and early 1970s.

As my anxiety and confusion mounted, Lillian appeared as an improbable angel to rescue me. Her interest in me had persisted. After her boyfriend had taken off to a mine in the far northwest of Australia, she sought me out, unaware of the depth of my problems.

My life changed radically. My sexual confusion, as I saw it, was resolved; Lillian was unfazed by my crushes, which I disclosed to her, but which she didn't take seriously – 'the world of fantasy and imagination knows no moral dimension', she told me. 'I sometimes fantasise about women. You're just inexperienced.' Our sexual relationship was brief, but the bond of trust was to remain for a lifetime.

Her life was chaotic and challenging, imaginatively extraordinarily rich, full of humour, and behind her streetwise toughness, a kind of innocence and vulnerability, and a deep capacity for affection and tenderness.

Lillian and Tim, 2005

She had boundless love for animals and plants; she introduced me to the pleasures of cats and gardening. And there was a deeper, profoundly painful side. Her parents were both the sole Holocaust survivor of their families in Poland, and she was their only child. They had moved to Israel when Lillian was three, and when she was ten they moved to Australia. She was a Yiddish speaker (this was the family language, which she maintained with her father until he died). She had had all her primary schooling in Hebrew in Israel, but unconsciously suppressed her knowledge of Hebrew after her arrival in Australia, a traumatic response to the anti-Semitism she experienced at school in Melbourne. Lillian introduced me to words from the 'strange' languages she knew, Yiddish and Hebrew. Lillian's childhood, as she narrated it, was a place of comfort imaginatively for me, so other, so innocent, so intimate, filled with warmth and humour, yet with poignancy and pain. When I was twenty-five, Lillian took me to Israel for the first time, and on our way there, in Greece, I remember the exquisite moment when she gave me my first lesson in the Hebrew alphabet, using the sand of an island beach as her writing tablet. It felt as if I were being reborn, as if the slate of my life had been wiped clean and I could start again. I began now to have a very different emotional understanding of the Jewish world from the one associated with the anti-Semitism of my culture: it represented life. But I was not entirely free; I experienced guilt and sometimes fear as I broke away from the patterns of my earlier life into this dangerous, very different world.

The course my life had now taken was incomprehensible to my family. My relationship with Lillian attracted enormous disapproval, and the underlying anti-Semitism became disturbingly overt. The fact that I had abandoned my faith, the first in the extended family of twenty-five first cousins to do so, that I had moved out of home before marriage (also a first), that I was now living in sin, and with a Jewish woman, that I had written an article for the student newspaper speculating about the possibility of sexual abuse at my junior school, that I was marching in 'communist' anti-war demonstrations – all this was too much for my mother, who had initially responded with concern and sympathy to my emotional problems. 'The only thing that prevents me from thinking that you are evil is that you are my son,' she said one day, after a visit from her very censorious older sister, a nun. My father was no better: a couple of years after the worst of my emotional crisis, in a discussion at the dinner table over the suicide of the daughter of close friends of theirs, in which I was critical of the parents, my father defensively remarked: 'If you had killed yourself a couple of years ago, none of us would have known why.'

I was temporarily cut out of my parents' will.

*

Who, then, was Paul, so unlike my own father?

Paul's warmth and generous spirit shaped our relationship; he mentored us. Pat was one of only two children of the surviving members of Paula's family, born after the war, and there were none on Paul's side. Paul had always shown his fondness for Pat on his occasional visits to New York as she was growing up, and he extended this to us, her friends, when she came to Melbourne to live with him for a time. We were the future, the opposite of the losses he had experienced. He had a quiet seriousness and an intensity, reflecting a moral vision and a disciplined quality that occasionally tended to severity, though mostly he was very tolerant and indulgent of us. We responded enthusiastically to his wisdom and to his vast knowledge of and curiosity about the world, and about history, science and literature. We were innocent young Australians, idealistic and naive, and he taught us.

He had an old-fashioned idea of travel. (I had never travelled outside Australia.) He advised us always to tip the head waiter on arrival in a restaurant, to ensure good service. (I had never been to a restaurant and didn't know how I would identify a head waiter.) He was impatient with the casualness with which people travelled in the age of mass tourism – he considered it important for a traveller to read about the history and culture of the place they were visiting. (Accordingly, I now have on my bookshelves the histories of many countries I have visited.) 'When I visit a new city, I always go to the poorest part of the city; you can tell from the condition of the poorest areas what the society is like,' he explained.

Paul listened to us as we earnestly discussed what we were reading, thinking, the turbulent politics of the day, the profound cultural shift and sexual revolution that was going on. There was a hint of amusement as he listened: compared to what he had experienced growing up in Vienna during World War I, and as a student and young engineer through the violent political atmosphere and the cultural and sexual upheavals in the 1920s and 1930s, it was hard for him to take our enthusiasms too seriously. He talked to us about politics, about Marxism, about the environment. He saw Jewish civilisation as representing, at its best, an advancement of human consciousness. He had visited Israel once, and the only comment he made to us was that he was struck by how people in a crowded bus would stand up for him, a small, older Jewish man. Of course, he had attitudes characteristic of his age. He had a particular view of what he saw as the eternal truth, independent of the ideology of a particular age, of the relations between men and women, encapsulated for him in Rodin's famous statue *Eternal Idol*, in which the man physically worships the woman, who is slightly elevated above him. He was intolerant of homosexuality and had old-fashioned views on physical discipline. But these didn't affect my trust in him. His manner with us was always warm and encouraging. There was a deep grief and a sense of despair in him. I remember he went to see Bertolucci's *Last Tango in Paris* three times in the cinema. The film is a study of visceral grief following the loss of a wife, and it is known that Brando's own wounds were fully exposed in the making of that film.

Paul's life at the same time posed profound challenges. His question to me – 'You Catholics believe that we Jews killed God' – was only one aspect of that challenge. Intellectually, but also emotionally, I understood how significant the question was, as at the time he posed it I had been involved in the years-long intellectual search to understand the basis for my Catholic faith, which was also the key to my identity, my family culture and my attitude to my sexuality. My first response was strong denial, and shock that he could suggest this. I slowly began to realise that it had relevance for the Holocaust, and specifically as experienced by him and his family, as the question targeted the source of anti-Semitism in Christianity. I began to think seriously about the significance of anti-Semitism for Christianity, and hence as one of the foundations our culture. Years later, at a lecture by a visiting eminent historian of the Holocaust, a Catholic nun, I was struck to see her acknowledgement that (in her words) 'Christianity was a necessary but not sufficient condition for the Holocaust'.

A troubling aspect of this challenge was the recognition of my own anti-Semitism, and that of my family and culture. I was exposed to anti-Semitism, and socialised into it, throughout my childhood. We didn't know any Jews, but we knew about them, and were reminded of the Gospels' representation of their role in Christ's suffering and death, in our religious education at school, and in the liturgy. This was most dramatically illustrated during the solemn service on Good Friday: a public holiday in Melbourne, when all the shops were closed, no public activities such as sporting events permitted, the streets deathly quiet, like no other day. The religious drama of the day was enacted in the afternoon at the local parish church. The only service of the day was at the unusual time of 3 pm, the time of Christ's death according to the Gospels, and was not a Mass, the only day in the year on which Mass was not said; it was also a day of fasting, one of only two such days in the year. Instead, inside the church, the tabernacle, in which was kept the host (the consecrated bread embodying – literally, in our belief – the physical body of Christ), was thrown open, shockingly empty; the religious images on the walls of the church were covered; the priest wore black vestments as he conducted the service (only otherwise worn at funerals). I was intensely involved in the profound symbolism of the day. In the long afternoon service, readings from St John's Gospel included Pilate's offer of Jesus to the Jewish crowd ('the Jews'), who rejected him, shouting, 'Crucify him, crucify him'; the priest led us in prayer for the conversion of 'the perfidious Jews'.

An incident one Saturday afternoon showed how deeply this conditioning had shaped me, even as a young child. I was ten. Each Saturday, the whole family would pile into Dad's iconic FJ Holden and head off to Junction Oval, the home ground of our team, St Kilda. Loyalty to St Kilda was ingrained in our family culture: even my mother had 'converted' from supporting her club, South Melbourne (where she was born), when she married Dad. We made our way through the turnstiles into the members' section; Mum, my aunt and her mother with their rugs and thermos headed into the stand to sit down; the men stood near the fence, closer to the action. I was thought to bear a resemblance to one of the best-known players in the team, and so the die-hard women fans sitting on the fence ushered me down a bit closer to the action – 'little Billy Young', they said, a kind of mascot. St Kilda, as usual, was not doing well. As the game proceeded, I became aware of a middle-aged man with dark features standing near me watching the game, gesticulating strangely. Was he putting some kind of jinx or spell on the St Kilda players? In a sudden frightened moment of clarity, I thought that he must be a Jew! (He was probably suffering from something like Tourette's Syndrome, my adult self understands). Anti-Semitism, like football, was in our blood, in my blood at least, 'in my mother's milk'.

Anti-Semitic references were part of everyday life. Mum's brother, and also one of Dad's very closest friends, would greet my father good-humouredly with, 'How are you going, you hook-nosed Jewish bastard?' My mother referred to someone as 'a Jewy sort of fellow'. My schoolfriend Mick Adams was dating a girl called Margaret Bloom. Despite the fact that Margaret was Catholic, attending a Catholic girls' school and her mother was Catholic, her father was Jewish, and this was a big problem for Mick's mother, Mary Adams. Mary forbade Mick from dating her. The solution was to invite me along so it couldn't be considered a date – I would agree to go out with Mick on Saturday night; we would swing by Margaret's house to pick her up, and then go to see a drive-in movie, not very comfortable for any of us. In the end Mick broke up with Margaret. I think Mary Adams had her way: the pressure was too great.

I kept feeling the pressure, too, to my shame, even with Paul. I couldn't simply shake off the anti-Semitism of my culture, which I had deeply internalised; though I rejected it totally intellectually, and as part of my love for Lillian and Paul, on some very deep level it maintained a residual hold on me, through guilt about the path that I had taken, and it was fed by my underlying anxiety about my sexuality too. I recognised with shock that psychologically I was like the weak Fascist lead character in Bertolucci's 1970 film *The Conformist*, which I watched with Lillian; he was also conflicted about his sexuality. I knew I was weak, and a coward, afraid of rebelling against the family and its values, and only my trust of Lillian, like a thread guiding me through the labyrinth, would enable me to rebuild my life and not succumb to the pressures of my old world and the clash I felt between the values of the two cultural worlds – my anti-Semitic Catholic family and the Jewish world of Paul and Lillian.

This clash of worlds that I was experiencing found expression symbolically in the choice that I made on that evening in 1973 between my father and Paul as a father figure. I knew that Paul was, of course, not my real father, and the failure of my relationship with my father is a source of pain and regret, as it was never resolved before his death. I loved him and needed him; I know he loved me – my mother was more perceptive, and very intelligent, but she was impatient, and I turned to Dad for warmth, like on that Caulfield Cup Day when I was a young child and we were gardening together. But his drinking incapacitated him and as I reached a crisis in my own life, he could do nothing, and finally turned on me in response to my rejection of him and the family values. Three weeks after the birthday party that I didn't attend, I left with Lillian for Paris, and in the course of the next ten years in London my life changed forever.

Tim McNamara, 1970s

Chapter 2

Vienna

It was summer and I had been in London for two years. Paul was on his way to Vienna to visit his sister, Olga, and invited me to come with him. But young and thoughtless as I was, I chose instead a beach holiday that I had planned on a Greek island.

Years later after Paul's death, I felt that there was no point in seeing Vienna on my own, as I had missed my chance to see it with Paul as my guide. But then, in 2005, an academic invitation gave me a chance to be in Vienna; not a sight-seeing visit, which seemed pointless and somehow indecent, but it was an opportunity to begin an exploration of Paul's past, thirty years after his death. It was such a short visit, and the days were taken up with academic commitments, that I had to do most of my exploration in the evening. I focused on the addresses Pat had given me where Paul and Paula had lived. In the near darkness, I sought out one of the most important: Novaragasse 39 in Leopoldstadt, where I knew Paul had grown up. There was a plaque on the apartment building and I imagined it might give a clue as to the building's history in the war. It was in German, so I took photos; I later learnt that the plaque was identical to thousands of others in Vienna, documenting the dates of the reconstruction of individual buildings following bomb damage during the war, placed as records of the achievements of the socialist governments in the 1950s and 1960s. It was not what I had hoped it might be. I was groping in the dark and realised what a challenge it would be to get some understanding of his life and world in this unfamiliar city.

A year later, I was invited to visit the university in Vienna again, this time for a stay of four months. I accepted: it was a chance to engage with Paul's world in depth. I arrived on a balmy day in September, in time for the start of the new academic year. One of my hosts kindly met me at the airport and we headed for my accommodation, which turned out to be in Leopoldstadt. We were soon driving along a tree-lined road parallel to the Danube Canal (Donaukanal), a branch of the Danube skirting the old city of Vienna, the 1st district. The trees looked lovely; the buildings we passed were so distinctively European – and beautiful. My flat on Hollandstrasse was only a few metres from the canal. From the window of the flat, I could see the oldest church in Vienna, the medieval Ruprechtskirche, St Ruprecht's, and the spire of Stephansdom, St Stephen's, the famous Vienna cathedral, in the centre of the old city.

I had come to Vienna with mixed feelings and expectations – on the one hand, the compelling project of connecting with Paul, but on the other, the scepticism that this mission was romantic, sentimental. Within a few days of being there I felt an intense closeness to Paul. I experienced a sudden and powerful emotional realisation: it was as if he were giving me the city, its beauty and richness, and its pain, as his gift. Every street, every stone of the buildings in Vienna made me feel a deep, nurturing connection with him. A naive outsider from the new world, I was finally fulfilling his wish, like a dutiful son, that I would discover his city, discovering what his life there had been and had meant, trying to peel away the layers of forgetting, and my own ignorance, to understand the sadness and grief that prevented him from ever living here again. What evidence could I find, to help me understand? What ensued for me in those four months and in the years following was an unfolding and continuing process of discovery. Paul's world slowly but compellingly revealed itself to me.

I began in Leopoldstadt. I learnt that Jewish settlement occurred there in two separate periods. A Jewish community had arrived in the area before 1670 but was expelled in that year by the Emperor Leopold I, and the district was renamed Leopoldstadt in his honour, the very name a testimony to rampant anti-Semitic feeling at that time. Ironically, some two centuries later, in a period of rapid industrialisation and monumental building in Vienna known as the *Gründerzeit*, Leopoldstadt became synonymous with the significant, mostly poor, growing Jewish population who had come from other parts of the empire: Bohemia, Moravia and (further east) Galicia and Bukovina. It came to be known by the nickname *die Mazzesinsel* (Matzo Island).

The many narrow streets of Leopoldstadt were often silent, with relatively little vehicle or foot traffic, and the buildings imposing. The older buildings were in the *Gründerzeit* style, a heavier version of Haussmann's Paris. Four to seven storeys high, mostly in neutral stone colours, some painted in pastels, or more recently in brighter colours; the facades elaborately decorated in the ornate taste of the time. Despite their often grand facades, these were the tenements that housed the Jewish families, most of whom were poor. They might have a decorated lobby, sometimes even a carriageway, and curved wrought-iron staircases, sometimes there would be a courtyard with trees, but more often it was just a place for rubbish bins.

At Novaragasse 39, in a street beyond the creeping gentrification of the area, I found the building where Paul had lived as a child. The heavy door was open, and I entered – in front was a curved staircase hidden partly by a pillar, an old ornate tap for getting water near the ground, and in the opening as the stairs climbed, delicate ironwork details, and an old light fitting, now with just a bare bulb. It had a shabby feel, with discarded children's bicycles and tricycles stacked under the stairs, and angry reminders on a noticeboard nearby about not littering. I climbed the staircase to the first floor – a narrow corridor, the floor damaged and crudely repaired, bars on the windows of flats, heavy double doors of the flat at the end painted a dull dark brown. This was an immigrant area, again. Outside, I could see in the distance beyond Novaragasse the Riesenrad, the giant Ferris wheel, which is the great symbol of Vienna, and which features ominously in *The Third Man*, on permanent showing at a cinema on the Ringstrasse. There was a melancholy feeling in this street, in this building.

Where was the past, apart from in the buildings themselves? I looked for external signs, explicit acknowledgement of the city's awareness of its past, of the context and violent events that had shaped Paul's life.

I came across a telling memorial one day, early in my time exploring Leopoldstadt. In Alexander-Poch-Platz, a short street in front of the parish church of St Leopold, I learnt the origin of the name of the square – a plaque had been installed in honour of a much-loved priest:

> Dr Alexander Poch
> parish priest of St Leopold's, 1938–1966
> spiritual father of the community
> helper of people oppressed in hard times
> re-builder of the church destroyed during the war.

Vienna

St Leopold's, the church of which Dr Poch was parish priest, bore an elaborate Latin inscription above the portal. I drew on my rusty Latin to slowly decipher bits of it. The inscription refers to the consecration of the church in 1671, built in celebration of the expulsion of the Jews 'from the whole of Lower Austria' and the destruction of their synagogue with its 'vices' the previous year. The plaque celebrates the architects of this violence, Emperor Leopold I and his wife, Margarita, (the Infanta at the centre of Velasquez's *Las Meninas* and an anti-Semite). The synagogue, which had been built some thirty years earlier, had been pulled down and replaced by this consecrated church, built under the patronage of the city of Vienna and its mayor, Daniel Springer. (This church was, in turn, replaced by a larger church in 1722.) A modern plaque from the Vienna Tourist Board explained the main point, albeit briefly (and, unusually, also in English):

> In 1670, Emperor Leopold I expelled
> the Jewish Viennese and commissioned
> a church instead of a synagogue.
> New church built 1722–24.

I entered the church vestibule: the church was usually closed on weekdays, although you could see into the body of the church through a glass wall screening the vestibule from the church proper, which like many churches in Vienna was elaborately baroque. An elderly parishioner sitting in the vestibule greeted me, asking me in English why I had come. I mentioned the problematic origin of the church, as indicated by the text over the entrance, and commented that there seemed to be little acknowledgement of the history of the church in the pamphlets available in the vestibule. 'Well, the Jews caused a lot of trouble,' she replied, and explained that the church had been bombed during the war, and its roof had caved in. I now understood the significance for this parishioner of the tribute to Dr Poch in the plaque in the square outside as 're-builder of the church destroyed during the war'. Why was she ignoring his reputation as a person who had helped victims of Nazism ('helper of men suffering in hard times')? These had included Jews who were now confessional Catholics but classified as Jews under the Nuremberg Laws, and vulnerable others. Dr Poch had even been briefly arrested by the Nazi authorities.

Throughout Leopoldstadt I kept coming across memorials not to what had happened 'in hard times' but celebrating the efforts of the social democratic governments in the postwar years to rebuild the area. Leopoldstadt had been heavily damaged, as it was on the frontline of the battle for Vienna between the Russian and German armies. I found small plaques over the entrances of older buildings whose war damage had been repaired by the city government, or lettered signs on the walls of *Gemeindebauten*, social housing, dating from the 1950s, 1960s and 1970s, echoing the style developed in Red Vienna in the 1920s and 1930s. Plain, unadorned apart from proud announcements of the date of the construction or restoration, they were a reminder to the public that, as in Red Vienna, it had been the democratic socialist government that had been responsible for the construction of these buildings.

Even where acknowledgement of Nazi violence was made, it seemed that it had been easier for the city in the postwar period to erect plaques emphasising the socialist resistance to the Nazis rather than the horror of the fate of its Jewish population. I learnt that Leopoldstadt was in the Soviet Occupation Zone until 1955 and reflected the

Stalinist policy of not distinguishing among the victims of Nazism, and emphasising communist resistance. For example, in Novaragasse 17–19, a plaque erected by the city in 1953 to the communist journalist Alfred Klahr (who was Jewish) memorialised his resistance activities:

> Here lived Dr Alfred Klahr
> He was murdered by the SS-Fascists during the
> Nationalist Socialist regime in July 1944, aged 39 years.
> He fought for a free, democratic Austria, for peace,
> and for the happiness of mankind. May people
> recognise his sacrifice.

A plaque with identical wording, again erected by the City of Vienna in 1953, at Schiffamtsgasse 18–20, honoured Dr Arnold Deutsch. Deutsch, another communist (also Jewish), was the Soviet agent who recruited Philby, Burgess, Maclean and other spies in the 1930s in England, where he had fled; the circumstances of his death are disputed, though it seems likely he died in the torpedo sinking of a boat crossing the Atlantic.

It was left to the small remnant Jewish community in the postwar years to commemorate the Jewish past of Leopoldstadt and its annihilation in the Holocaust. The sporadic reminders of Jewish fates I encountered on signs and memorials were not many, and there were few physical signs otherwise of the prewar Jewish presence in the area. I learnt the reason: the almost 100 Jewish institutional buildings in Vienna destroyed on Kristallnacht on the night of 9–10 November 1938 had been replaced by other buildings, and no indication had been left of what had been there before. Vienna contrasts with Prague, I discovered on a visit there later: Prague was occupied by German forces only after Kristallnacht, and its many Jewish buildings, now typically museums or other kinds of tourist sites, are still preserved, although again there are few Jews living there. I had with me the book *Jewish Vienna* to guide my search, tracing the fates of synagogues: the Leopoldstädter Temple in Tempelgasse, the Turkish Temple in Zirkusgasse, Schiffschul in Grosse Schiffgasse, the Polish Shul in Leopoldgasse, the Pazmaniten Temple in Pazmanitengasse, their locations left unmarked by the city. Occasionally, there were community commemorative plaques with inscriptions in Hebrew and German, translated as:

> Here stood the Polish Synagogue,
> built in 1892/93 following the plans of the architect
> Wilhelm Stiassny, destroyed in the 'Kristallnacht'
> pogrom on November 10th, 1938.

In Pazmanitengasse, a sign in German and Hebrew read:

> Here stood the former Pazmaniten Synagogue.
> It was destroyed in the Kristallnacht pogrom on
> November 10th, 1938. Jewish Community of Vienna.

Particularly egregious individual examples of brutality were sometimes recorded. Under a Star of David, I found the following in Förstergasse:

> On April 12th, 1945, a few hours before the liberation
> of Vienna from the Nazi tyranny,
> Dr Blum Nelly, 54 years   Klüger-Langer Grete, 44 years
> Holzer Arthur, 59 years   Margolin Marie, 44 years

Vienna

> Klein Arthur, 56 years   Mezei Kurt, 21 years
> Klüger-Langer Erna, 82 years   Pfeiffer Emil, 66 years
> Schaier Genia, 48 years
> were murdered in front of this building by ruthless
> barbarians of the SS. Never forget!
> Jewish Community of Vienna.

The lack of memorialisation by the city was highlighted when I encountered other official memorials. I came across a plaque commemorating Fritz Kreisler, 'violin virtuoso and composer, born here on 2nd March 1875', probably dating from his centenary in 1975. But even this was selective: Jewish prewar figures in literature and politics were seldom mentioned – there was nothing to indicate where the Jewish novelist Joseph Roth lived, on Rembrandtstrasse; or Theodor Herzl, the founder of Zionism, on Taborstrasse; or the Nobel Prize-winning Sephardic Jewish novelist and memoirist Elias Canetti, on Haidgasse.

This absence, this erasure, was also true of the buildings used as collection camps (*Sammellager*) where Jewish families, removed from their homes, had to spend time in cramped quarters prior to deportation. An exhibition in 2007 of the history of these buildings stated: 'The path to destruction began in the middle of the city. Kleine Sperlgasse 2a, Castellezgasse 35, Malzgasse 7 and 16 – these addresses in Vienna's Leopoldstadt are hardly present in Austria's collective memory. In the topography of the Shoah, however, they are central places.' The largest and most important of these *Sammellager* was the one at Kleine Sperlgasse 2a, which used to be a school. I was to find out later that this building, adjacent to Paul's high school, was where Paul's mother, Mathilde, and Paula's friend Martha had been held and from which they had been deported to Theresienstadt. Following the end of the deportations, Malzgasse 7 became a small *Altersheim* (aged care home); it was here that Paula had worked as a nurse.

I now stood in front of Kleine Sperlgasse 2 and imagined it as a school, with cheerful banners. I found a dark metal plaque dating from 1984 on the external wall (again, a private memorialisation) acknowledging the history of the building:

> In memory
> of the 40,000 Jewish fellow citizens who,
> in the period from October 1941 to March 1943,
> were held by the Gestapo in this section of the school,
> and from here were deported to extermination camps.
> Never forget.

There was another memorial tablet at this school, installed in 2006, one of many which I came across as I walked the silent, melancholy streets of Leopoldstadt. These *Stolpersteine*, 'stumbling blocks', small square brass plaques fixed into the pavement or onto the walls of buildings, commemorate deportations and murders. This one read:

> In memory
> of the approximately 45,000 Jewish people
> who spent their last days in terrible conditions in this
> collection camp, before being deported.

Often the *Stolpersteine* are at the last known residence of individual Jews deported from Vienna, giving the names, dates and fate of the victims. In the pavement on Förstergasse I saw:

> In this house lived for many years
> Pessie Chary (Aunt Pepi)
> 11.06.1876,
> deported to Lagów
> on 12.3.1941.
> Murdered.

I learnt from friends in Leopoldstadt that the decision to commemorate the lives of these victims was not without dispute. Just one resident could oppose and there would be no memorial: my landlady said that a resident of her building on Herminengasse had objected, and so a proposed commemoration of victims who had lived at the address could not go ahead. This policy of introducing a right of opposition was initiated by the city. Gunter Demnig, the German artist who in Cologne in 1996 initiated the *Stolpersteine* project, wanted to place plaques in Vienna, as he had already done in cities around Europe, but the authorities required him to obtain the consent of the residents of each building before the stones could be installed. Nevertheless, since 2005, over 1000 *Stolpersteine* have been installed in Vienna. A *Weg der Erinnerung* (Path of Remembrance) now guides the visitor.

Thus, as the decades have passed, it seems to have become easier for some Viennese to engage in public memory work to acknowledge the violent history of the district. I came across more examples at Rembrandtstrasse 33, where the residents of the building had recently erected a plaque at the entrance with the names of the twenty-seven Jewish residents who were '*vertrieben, deportiert, ermordet*' ('evicted, deported, murdered') between 1938 and 1945. Place names could become memorials: a street sign marking Lancplatz explained that Maria and Dr Arthur Lanc had rescued three Hungarian Jews from a concentration camp, and in

1986 had been honoured as 'Righteous among the Gentiles'. Rabbiner-Friedmann-Platz commemorated Israel Friedmann (1854–1933), a Rabbi whose house of prayer was destroyed during Kristallnacht.

I discovered, however, that even such recent efforts of memorialising could be subsequently obscured. In 2014, *Das Mahnmal Alltagsskulpturen* (The Everyday Sculpture Memorial) by the young artist Catrin Bolt began to appear. In certain locations in Leopoldstadt and elsewhere, fragments of poignant texts, quotations from the testimony of victims of violence in the area, were placed at locations named in the texts. The texts were inscribed in capital letters in the pavement stone. My initial encounter was sometimes puzzling when I came across the testimony in mid-text. I needed to walk along the length of the text to understand it; some quotations were quite long. For example, Grosse Pfarrgasse, as its name ('Great Parish Street') suggests, runs next to the parish church of St Leopold. Here, immediately adjacent to the church, I came across a quotation extending for 200 or 300 metres along the street, recording the poignant experience of a grandmother living in Pfarrgasse parting with her son Poldi at the time of the forced emigration in the late 1930s, I later found out in my research. There was little chance of a woman of her age getting a visa. The original text read:

> So Poldi, who'd scarcely been any further than nearby places like Kaltenleutgeben[1] or Znaim[2] or, once in his childhood, as far as Abbazia[3], and was the most inept person imaginable

---

1 A spa town in the Vienna Woods about 20km from Vienna.
2 A country town just over the border in the Czech Republic, now Znojmo, 90km from Vienna.
3 Now Opatija, on the Adriatic coast in Croatia, formerly in the Habsburg Empire, part of the Austrian Riviera; 500km from Vienna.

as a traveller, set out on a journey across the great ocean. His last day and evening (night) before leaving he spent with us so that it was easier for Grandma, with whom he had lived his whole life. He simply left her (on the surface, of course). It was as usual, except that a single sentence that he always said was missing; which was, when he was supposed to be back. She stood by the kitchen window, as usual, when one of her children was expected; Grandma always stood by the window half an hour ahead of time and looked up Pfarrgasse towards Taborstrasse, where at Kaffee Niebauer the O-, C- or V-tram stopped, which took you past the pastry shop into the city, or to the Schwedenplatz tram.

Yet the text, as I encountered it, was not exactly like this and appeared to make no sense. Several sections of it had been removed where the pavement had been dug up and replaced – presumably for cabling, pipes or similar local infrastructure work. It now read:

> She stood by the kitchen window, as usual, when one of her children was ex_____d; Grandma always stood by the window half an hour a____me and looked up Pfarrgasse towards Taborstrasse, where at Kaffee Niebauer ____ C- or V-tram stopped, which took you past _____ into the city _____.

I came across the moving testimony of a witness to and victim of the violence of Kristallnacht in the pavement at Im Werd, at the corner of Schiffamtsgasse and Leopoldsgasse, near the site of a destroyed Orthodox Jewish school:

I came to the corner of Leopoldgasse and Malzgasse, and now heard for myself the terrible roar of our school being destroyed. The teachers had been beaten up and the Principal, Joel Pollak, was lying in a pool of blood. They had kicked him in the face and his nose was broken and he was unconscious. I turned round immediately, and with the children streaming past, I wanted to go home. At the double. Because the Hitler Youth were chasing us. I ran; behind me were the Hitler Youth. I ran through Im Werd, which is a short street. An 'Aryan' coal merchant had his business here, two doors from the Jewish butcher. The coal merchant sees me coming, and he trips me up. I fall, and the Hitler Youth throw themselves on me. They beat me up, I scramble to my feet and run.

On more recent visits, when I was staying with friends on Herminengasse, I noticed a new memorial, dating from 2017. At the U2 underground station at Schottentor, the German artist Michaela Melián has created murals on either wall of a short tunnel leading to the Herminengasse exit. The work commemorates the fate of the 800 Jewish men, women and children who either lived on Herminengasse or were confined there in the period 1938–1945 and were subsequently deported and murdered. Each tunnel wall represents one side of the street; the length of the tunnel has simple black-and-white sketch representations of the buildings. Each building is connected by one or more grey lines to an alphabetical list of the concentration camps to which the residents of the building were deported, the lists of camps sitting at the end of each tunnel wall. The work, whose grey lines resemble a rail network, thus manages to represent the individual fate of the inhabitants of each building, in a cumulative and powerful way. Thousands of commuters pass through the passage containing the mural each day, a routine reminder of the past; the routineness no doubt dulls the memory, but the provocation of the mural remains.

And what of individual memory? Friends living in the 2nd and 9th districts (the 9th another former Jewish area, where professionals tended to live; Freud's apartment is there) were aware that the apartments in which they lived, with their elegant, large rooms, high ceilings and parquet floors, had borne witness to the fates of the families who previously lived there.

A retired colleague from the university and his wife, who were very kind to me in Vienna, told me a story: they had been at home one day in one such gracious apartment in an older building on Grosse Sperlgasse in Leopoldstadt when the doorbell rang – an unfamiliar voice, could she and her father come up, as he had lived in the flat before the war and wanted to see it again. Yes, of course, come up. The father was very moved to see his old family home. His family had been forced into exile and had managed to make it to the United States; he had been a boy at the time. My friends invited the man and his daughter to dinner the following evening, an invitation which was gladly accepted, but the daughter phoned the following day and said that her father had been very emotional after the visit; she thanked my friends for their kindness but said that they were reluctantly declining the dinner invitation.

I personally felt this friend's sympathetic engagement with my own memory project. Below the *Stolperstein* to Pessie Chary, mentioned earlier, lies an inscription:

> But in Auschwitz
> love couldn't save you,
> and neither could reason
> —Ruth Klüger

I learnt that the quote was from the well-known memoir by Ruth Klüger called *Weiter Leben* (Living On). Outside a small shop on Taborstrasse, one of the main thoroughfares of Leopoldstadt, I came across copies of the book lying in a remainder bin. I went in and in my clumsy German asked to buy one; the shopkeeper said I could have it for free. It seemed the copies were being discarded: the book was too familiar, perhaps studied too often at school. In the window of a bookshop elsewhere on Taborstrasse several similar, but less well-known, memoirs by refugees and survivors were displayed; a section of the shop featured these. I mentioned the story of the Klüger book to the friend who had told me the story of his visitor. We had dinner together a few days later; he gave me copies of two memoirs of people who had lived in Leopoldstadt and had been forced into exile; I recognised one from the window of the bookshop. Such individual acts of remembrance meant so much, in the general silence of Leopoldstadt.

*

I have noticed on my visits to Vienna over a period of now fifteen years that Leopoldstadt is changing, as 'bobos' move in, and cafes and restaurants appear; there is a line of gentrification, moving steadily outward. One of my favourite places in Leopoldstadt is the Saturday morning farmers market at Karmelitermarkt, near where I have stayed with friends; people queue to buy fresh fruit and vegetables, flowers, preserves, jams, cheeses, bread and cakes, or to eat and have coffee at the brunch places around the edges of the market. The scene becomes busier and more elegant on each of my visits. Since the late 1970s, a small Jewish community has established itself in Leopoldstadt, Jews from Russia who arrived in Vienna as a staging post on their way out; some of them decided to stay instead of moving on to Israel or the United States, as most did. They are mostly religious and originally from the Caucasus, very unlike the worldly secular Jews of prewar Vienna, and more like the kaftan-wearing, Yiddish-speaking *Ostjuden* (Eastern Jews) who had so embarrassed the assimilated Viennese Jews in Paul's time. Gentrification and the sheer passage of time are putting the final seal on forgetting, as the present is made beautiful and the 'inconvenient' past is slowly, finally for the most part, erased – except for where it can't be.

I discovered on my walks in Leopoldstadt a beautiful park, the Augarten, an eighteenth-century formal park in the French style with avenues of chestnut and lime trees. The park has a long and complex history, initially established by Emperor Leopold I in the seventeenth century, and home in the eighteenth and early nineteenth centuries to concerts by Mozart, Beethoven and Schubert. It houses the Imperial Porcelain Factory and the training school of the Vienna Boys' Choir. What could be more Viennese? Indeed. In the centre of the park is an incongruous, many would say grotesque, ineradicable reminder of the Nazi past – a *Flakturm*, a Flak Tower, one of eight built in German cities (Berlin, Hamburg and Vienna) from 1940 to shelter resources and personnel from Allied bombing. The one in the Augarten is one of the tallest, 54 metres high and 43 metres in diameter; it was only completed in January 1945, near the end of the war. The buildings, of concrete, were made to be indestructible, and so they are: an accidental detonation of tons of explosives inside in 1946 did not destroy the tower but broke windows in the neighbourhood. It is now a wart on the beauty of the park. Someone has painted on its side, in large capitals, in English: 'NEVER AGAIN'.

Paul and Paula

*

As I explored other parts of Vienna, I found examples of a similar ambivalence or reluctance to engage, in three important memorials to the war period that I discovered in the central part of the city, the Innere Stadt, the 1st district.

The first is the ugly memorial in Morzinplatz, near the Danube Canal. It lies in a park on the site of the former Hotel Metropole, which was used as the Gestapo headquarters; the building was destroyed in the last days of the war during the Battle of Vienna, and never rebuilt. The memorial dates from 1985, although its inscription is from a simpler monument erected by a socialist organisation of survivors in 1951. At the top of the monument is the admonition *'Niemals Vergessen'* ('Never forget') with an inverted red triangle on the left. This was the symbol in the camps used for political prisoners: social democrats, socialists, trade unionists, Freemasons, communists and anarchists. On the right is the yellow Star of David. The text reads:

> Here stood the headquarters of the Gestapo
> It was hell for those Austrians who knew it
> For many it was the forecourt of death
> It is now sunk into ruin
> Like the thousand-year Reich
> BUT AUSTRIA HAS RISEN
> And with it our dead, the immortal victims

The monument represents the events in purely political terms, reflecting the socialist ideology of the early 1950s. Its triumphalist and nationalist tone feels inappropriate for Holocaust memorials, despite the yellow star. In the street nearby is a small memorial to the victims of the war – again, largely political, with little explicit reference to Jewish victims. My perspective on the events of the Holocaust reflected in this monument was echoed by another visiting scholar with whom I shared an office at the university. A socialist, she objected to 'Jewish exceptionalism' in the commemoration of victims of the Nazis.

A second memorial, in Albertinaplatz, in the centre of old Vienna, near the Albertina Museum and the Opera House, dates from 1988, the fiftieth anniversary of the Anschluss. The square in which it is situated is dedicated to all the victims of the war indiscriminately, including of the Allied bombing, and even soldiers fighting for Hitler: the sculpture on the right shows a fallen Wehrmacht soldier with a steel helmet lying on the ground. The memorial also includes a controversial brutalist sculpture of a Jewish man on his knees scrubbing the pavement. I discovered that it refers to a famous image: in the days immediately following the Anschluss, Jews on their hands and knees were required to remove the painted slogans in the streets supporting continuing Austrian independence from Germany in the referendum planned but abandoned on the eve of the Anschluss. The inscription reads:

> By Alfred Hrdlicka
> Erected by the City of Vienna
> in the memorial year 1988
> In this place stood Philipphof
> which was destroyed in a bombing raid on 12th March 1945
> Hundreds of people who had sought refuge in the basement
> of the building lost their lives.
> THIS MEMORIAL IS DEDICATED TO ALL THE VICTIMS OF
> WAR AND FASCISM

In response to criticism of the Albertina Memorial by Simon Wiesenthal, the famous Holocaust survivor and so-called Nazi hunter, a memorial specifically for the Jewish victims of the Holocaust in Vienna by the British sculptor Rachel Whiteread was dedicated in 2000. I found it in a small square, Judenplatz, the site of a medieval synagogue destroyed in a pogrom of 1421; the square is surrounded on all sides by beautiful buildings from the seventeenth and eighteenth centuries, some restored. The sculpture is in concrete and has an external view of a large box-like room or bunker, meant to represent a library whose walls are made of books with their pages, rather than their spines, turned out. The double doors to the library are without handles, so they have an industrial feel; it reinforces the idea of enclosure, indeed of a gas chamber. It is conceptual art, and though it is intelligent, I found it had no Jewish feeling to it. Rachel Whiteread herself is not Jewish. In a talk I attended at the university by a German historian on the memorialisation of the Holocaust in Germany, I asked a question about my perception that in Vienna the evidence of the Holocaust was muted. 'Oh yes, you are right,' she said, 'the memorials in Vienna are encapsulated.'

I discovered that anxiety about commemorating Vienna's violent past is reflected in other things too, not just memorials. The city is full of wonderful music, another discovery on my visits. I had been invited by a colleague to a rehearsal of a choral 'Concert for Peace'; her mother was in the choir. The Vienna Symphony Orchestra was to be conducted by its famous, then resident conductor, Fabio Luisi. The concert took place in the Grosser Musikvereinssaal, one of Vienna's great venues for its musical culture. After an initial work on the theme of peace by a living Swiss composer, what followed was Schönberg's *A Survivor from Warsaw*, a short cantata based on an account from a

Holocaust survivor whom Schönberg had met. The spoken text relates an incident in a concentration camp. A group of older and ailing inmates, incapable of hurrying at reveille, have been beaten semi-conscious and left lying for dead. The officer demands that they rouse themselves and count out numbers in sequence, so that he can know exactly how many are to be sent to the gas chamber. This demand is repeated and repeated, ever faster. The narrator in this performance was the famous Austrian actor Maximilian Schell, the text mainly in English except for the barked commands of the officer. For those unfamiliar with the story and this work of Schönberg, as I was, the culmination of the work was startling. Suddenly, the inmates break into sung prayer, the Shema Yisrael, traditionally said by observant Jews as their last words. In this performance a male choir suddenly rose to their feet and began singing the prayer, in Hebrew. To suddenly hear this prayer in Hebrew as a moment in an invocation of the extremity of the Holocaust in that iconic setting in Vienna was overwhelming. It shook the conventional pieties of the concert to their foundation. Silence seemed the only appropriate response. In the premiere in Boston in 1946, the audience was silent for a full minute at the end of the performance, such was its impact. Instead, in this performance, without missing a beat, the conductor led the choir into the gentle Kyrie of Beethoven's Mass in C Major, a beautiful and calming work. The Holocaust was astonishingly, disturbingly present for a moment in this famous hall, but then immediately superseded by something familiar and reassuring. Any thought of Christianity's contribution to the Holocaust – 'a necessary but not sufficient condition for the Holocaust' – was thoroughly elided.

I discovered, too, that the history of Freud's apartment on Berggasse in the 9th district, now a museum, had a related significance. When I entered I felt that there was something haunting about it, a feeling of absence. The apartment building and the apartment itself are typical of those in the 9th district, where I learnt that the better-off Jewish professionals and businessmen often lived, with ornate winding staircases and elaborate lift shafts, courtyards, high ceilings, parquet floors. For two decades after the war the significance of the apartment was ignored; only in 1968, in response to pressure from the world psychiatric community, was the apartment purchased with government funds and in 1971 opened as a museum. But those hoping to see the famous couch or the furniture from the apartment will be disappointed – they were removed and taken to the Freud House in Hampstead London, where Freud fled in 1938. Anna Freud was asked if the furniture could be returned to Vienna. She refused. The absence of the furniture in Berggasse seemed eloquent.

I also came across, as I had seen in Leopoldstadt, instances of the revival of memory after a period of erasure. On my way to the university, I often walked along Wasagasse in the 1st district, where I passed a *Gymnasium* (academic high school) that featured in the writer Stefan Zweig's memoir about his childhood and youth in Vienna in the 1890s, *Die Welt von Gestern* (The World of Yesterday). I noticed a plaque acknowledging Zweig's attendance on the wall of the building, among other prominent alumni. I found the school open one day and went into the entrance hall. On one wall there was an older memorial listing the names of all the former students and teachers who had lost their lives fighting in the German army in Word War II. On the wall opposite was a more recent memorial plaque listing the names of the Jewish students and teachers who had been killed or driven into exile. I spoke about reading Zweig and my interest in the memorials in the school with a group of my students over drinks one evening after class. One of the students, a young woman, said she knew about the more recent memorial plaque – she had been a student at the school and one of the teachers there had known that there was only one memorial to those from the school who had died in the war, and it was to those who had fought for the Nazis. The teacher initiated a research project with student volunteers to try to discover the fate of the Jewish students and teachers who had been expelled; my student was one of the volunteers. The project had resulted in a book, which she gave me – stories of each of the survivors they had been able to find, many in the US, some of whom came to Vienna for the launch of the book. It also led to the memorial plaque. Such individual initiatives, I realised, played an important role in memory and memorialisation.

The previous year, on my first extended visit, I had been asked if I would give the Christmas lecture at the university. It was tradition for a guest professor to give a lighthearted lecture each year, in the last week before the Christmas break. I agreed, and took the task seriously, perhaps too seriously. There was a festive atmosphere: the technician, a composer and excellent but reluctant pianist, who had become a good friend, honoured me with a piano performance before the talk. The talk was entitled 'A journey into language: Ein Gastprof lernt Deutsch'. After some initial remarks about my halting early steps in learning German, I spoke about the context for my learning, my visit to Vienna. I showed a photograph of Paul and explained who he was, and that I was learning German to help me to engage more fully with Paul's language, and to read the poignant letters he had written to his family immediately before and after his departure from Vienna for England in late 1938. I showed excerpts from the letters, detailing the steadily worsening situation of those, like Paul's wife, Paula, left behind. I concluded this section of the talk by mentioning the irony of a poster I had seen in the U-Bahn, advertising the United Nations High Commission for Refugees (UNHCR). It showed a pair of tweezers removing the shell of a snail and talked about the high number of homeless refugees in the world. I commented that it was ironic to see this in a city that had sent 10 per cent of its citizens into exile at best, to their deaths at worst.

The final part of the lecture was again lighthearted, more 'fitting' to the occasion. Mostly those who had heard my talk were positive, certainly respectful; in discussions afterwards, one colleague told an anecdote about a Jewish friend of his mother's, a survivor, who had saved him from embarrassment and humiliation by persuading his provincial mother not to require him to wear lederhosen – traditional rural clothing – at his school in Vienna. One or two older people were clearly discomfited, or annoyed: 'Is there any need to bring this up?' one asked. One colleague who had a Jewish husband said, 'We rendered ourselves a stupid country because of what we did in the war,' she said. 'We killed off or exiled all the intelligent people and were left only with what remained.' It had felt right, though perhaps naive, to speak up for Paul in this public way; there was a sense of wanting to right the injustice done to the father.

The education that Paul had intended for me did not occur alone. It was as if I were feeling my way along a thread of continuity, bringing me into contact with people who could help things reveal themselves, help connections appear. One very significant friendship began in a wonderfully serendipitous way. Before one of my early visits to Vienna, I had spent a few days in London first, where I had seen a play by the Jewish playwright Ronald Harwood called *Collaboration*, which dealt with the issue of the collaboration of the composer Richard Strauss with the Nazi authorities. A few days later, I arrived in Vienna for a fortnight's visit. It was late June, my first summer in Vienna. Paul had told us that our education was not complete without an understanding of opera; he would have taken me to the Staatsoper if I had gone with him to Vienna in my youth. So, as on previous visits, in which I had managed to see Strauss's *Der Rosenkavalier* and Mozart's *Don Giovanni*, I checked out what was on at the Staatsoper. To my astonishment and delight, an opera currently in repertoire was *Die Schweigsame Frau*, the very work that was the subject of the play I had just seen in London. Not one of Strauss's best-known works, it was the first performance of the opera here in decades. I went to a well-known music shop I had discovered in the old city, bought a CD of the opera and listened to it non-stop in the days before the performance to familiarise myself with the music.

At the university a day or two later, I was invited to a discussion with a group of researchers who were working on language and asylum issues, an interest of mine. The head of the group, Brigitta Busch, and I immediately hit it off, and she invited me to lunch at her house the following day. Over lunch, as I explained my reasons for being in Vienna, I mentioned the remarkable coincidence that on this visit I was hoping to see the very Strauss opera that had been the subject of a play I had seen in London only a few days before. 'Thomas, tell Tim about your father,' Brigitta said to her husband. Thomas was the son by a second, late marriage of Adolph Busch, the famous German violinist who had made the painful, difficult decision no longer to perform in Germany after 1933, because his musical partner, Rudolf Serkin, the Jewish pianist, could no longer play. Busch had emigrated to Switzerland in 1927, and at the outbreak of war moved to Vermont in the United States, where he and Serkin set up the famous Marlboro Music School and Festival. He returned to Switzerland after the war, where Thomas was born. 'My father ended his friendship with Richard Strauss because of his public role in Nazi Germany,' Thomas said. I was struck by this extraordinary coincidence, of meeting someone who had a direct connection with the very issue that the play had been about, and moreover that touched on the themes I was exploring in Vienna. I managed to get a last-minute ticket to the opera. It turned out to be funny, tender and moving on the theme of ageing. And that was the beginning of a deep and lasting friendship with Brigitta and Thomas, who were unfailingly kind and supportive of my writing on my subsequent visits.

I benefitted from individual acts of kindness from others, too. At the time of my first visit to the university, I met someone who was to become a close friend, Paul B – a younger man, in his mid-thirties. The fact that he was also called Paul somehow oddly mattered to me, and a strange, deep trust developed between us. He offered to help me with my German, and I with his English – we would trade conversation. He was doing a PhD in industrial psychology, as well as training to be a gestalt therapist. He was interested in my story of Paul, and when we met for walks, he would often make a point of taking me somewhere with a Jewish interest – for example, once to Servitengasse in the 9th district to show me a memorial to the Jews who had lived in that particular street, among them Pat's own mother, Lilly. A privately initiated project had been undertaken in 2005–07 to tell the story of each of the Jewish families who had lived on the street in March 1938, the time of the Anschluss. Inset into the pavement was a large square of glass, under which were old-fashioned keys with labels carrying the names of residents. One year, Paul B moved into an apartment on the upper floor of a building on Schönbrunnergasse. From the windows of the apartment, he had a view onto the distinctive apartment building at Linke Wienzeile 158 in which Paul and Paula lived following their marriage until just before Paul's departure for England in April 1939. On one visit we went for a walk to inspect it. Paul B offered to 'keep an eye' on the building; he sent me regular reports on its wellbeing.

There were other acts of kindness, too, in support of my education in Vienna. I often reported what I had experienced in Vienna to Eva, a friend I had made in Melbourne, who had had a traumatic departure from Vienna as a child in 1938, first to the Bronx in New York, and then abruptly in the late 1940s to Melbourne. Eva was intrigued by my interest in Vienna. She told me that her family had lived in Leopoldstadt. On my first visit there I tracked down some of the places that she had mentioned. Her parents had had an apartment in the Dianabad in the 2nd district, in a fashionable apartment complex above a swimming pool, which was destroyed in the final months of the war. Her family owned a clothing shop on Taborstrasse; on my walks around Leopoldstadt, I realised that the shop was still there, now called Beged, which I recognised as a Hebrew word meaning clothes. The sign was somehow significant, as if there had been some sort of restitution, even if not in material terms. I reported to Eva what I had seen. She told me that relatives on her father's side, the Wolf family, wine merchants, had been prominent figures in Eisenstadt, the capital of Burgenland, on the Hungarian border south of Vienna. Accommodation in my first flat in Vienna, in Hollandstrasse, had been arranged by my new colleague, Barbara M, who, with her partner, Sigrid, became a friend. When Barbara and Sigrid heard Eva's story, they offered to take me to Eisenstadt. It turned out that Wolf house was now the Jewish Museum of Eisenstadt; an impressive building, but with an uninspiring collection of Jewish religious objects and not much history. With one very major exception – on the wall in one room was a framed copy of two pages from *Der Stürmer*, the Nazi magazine, attacking Eva's relative, Sándor Wolf. As I couldn't understand German, Sigrid took the trouble to translate the whole thing slowly for me (her English was not fluent). The violence of the text was extraordinary; it was a glimpse of the violence that Eva and her family had suffered until their escape.

Paul had wanted me to learn about Vienna and understand not only the context of the tragedy of his loss, but also the rich culture and intellectual and artistic history of the city he knew and had been forced to leave behind. My education about these riches had already begun when I had known him as a young man. I had been intrigued even then by his collection of prints by Egon Schiele and his interest in *Wozzeck*, the opera by Alban Berg, a production of which he had seen on a visit to Vienna a year or two before I met him. The opera, first performed in 1925, when Paul was twenty-four, adopts the atonal style of Schönberg, Berg's teacher. It presents a vision of the thin veneer between rationality and irrationality, and of the vulnerability of the weak and powerless in an unequal society.

I learnt that the intellectual and artistic environment into which Paul was born and grew up was marked by the emergence of the movement known as *Wiener Moderne* (Viennese Modernism), spanning the period from 1890 to World War I, and incorporating the Jugendstil (Art Nouveau) style. As I explored the streets of Vienna and went to its smorgasbord of galleries, museums and musical performances, I came to recognise its modernist aesthetic in architecture (Otto Wagner, Josef Hoffmann, Adolf Loos), design (Hoffmann and others), art (Gustav Klimt, Egon Schiele, Richard Gerstl) and music (especially Arnold Schönberg). I realised that Paul was thoroughly modernist in his sensibility. The building in which he and Paula lived following their marriage was in the Viennese Modernist style, the Litoralishof at Linke Wienzeile 158. Slowly, its interest, its beauty and its significance unfolded for me. Research and reading led me to understand something of the area. The Linke Wienzeile (literally, 'Left Vienna (River) Row') ran along the left side (*Linke*) of what had been the Vienna River (*Wienfluss*), which had been converted into an unattractive concrete channel in the late 1890s. The channel was redeemed by the beautiful stations and distinctive pale green railings of the underground line U4, which ran along it. They were part of the architect Otto Wagner's Stadtbahn, built in 1893–1901. The Stadtbahn was conceived as a kind of *Gesamtkunstwerk* ('total work of art'), in which all the elements – buildings, bridges, railings, lighting – were part of a coordinated design.

My initial exploration of Paul's building had been relatively unrevealing. The Linke Wienzeile, which extended as far as the Gürtel, the ring road around Vienna, was congested with traffic, and the surrounding area was impersonal. On a visit early in my time in Vienna, I had managed to slip inside the front door when someone was leaving the building, and had taken some photos of its elegant interior, but had no context within which to understand what I was seeing. And then, a guiding hand appeared. An archivist from the Technical University with whom I had been communicating about Paul's time as a student there sent a Google link to a picture of the building; he drew my attention to its name, Litoralishof – no doubt named as such because it was built on the banks of the Wienfluss. (*Litoral* in German can refer to the edges of rivers as well as lakes and the sea, unlike the English 'littoral'). I was intrigued by the design and history of the building. Its modernist features, particularly the tall, narrow front entrance, reminded me of some of the design features of the Wittgenstein House, designed by a student of the modernist architect Adolf Loos for the sister of the philosopher Ludwig, which I had seen on a visit with Thomas Busch. But attempts to find anything online about the architecture of the building, or its history, drew a blank. Brigitta and Thomas offered to investigate and managed to get inside. They reported: 'It is a really beautiful Jugendstil house. We rang several doorbells until a lady in the basement was so nice to open the door for us and let us take pictures in the inside. Many things do not seem to have changed since the time when Paul lived there.'

So, it was a Jugendstil/*Wiener Moderne* building, clearly significant, although Vienna has so many beautiful and distinctive buildings in this style that this building presumably only counted as a relatively minor one. My friend Paul B had found an entry about the building on an architectural history website, and suddenly the context in which the building had been designed and its aesthetic quality became clear. Litoralishof had been designed in 1910 by the brothers Carl and Adolf Stöger, and strongly reflected features of the new modernist architectural style of the Viennese architect and designer Josef Hoffmann. Carl Stöger, who had initially been trained in the prevailing historicist style, was a member of the Siebener Club (the Seven Club), a group of artists who met every Thursday nearby. When the club first formed in 1892 the original seven members involved leading figures from the famous Vienna Secession/Jugendstil movement, including Hoffmann. Carl Stöger became a member of the club and met Hoffmann, leading him to adopt the modernist ethic of Hoffman and other members of the Vienna Secession.

The rich aesthetic and historical significance of further buildings in the area around the Litoralishof continued to emerge. On the other side of the Wienzeile, I discovered another distinctive Jugendstil building, the Vorwärts-Gebäude (Forward Building) from 1909–10, designed by architect brothers who had trained under Otto Wagner. Here were located the offices of the Social Democratic party, led by Victor Adler until 1918, and of the publisher of the main Social Democratic newspaper, *Die Arbeiter-Zeitung*, until they were banned by the Austro-Fascist government following the brief civil war in Vienna in 1934. Trotsky, Bukharin and Lenin had visited Adler there.

I began to read widely on the intellectual and artistic culture in Vienna when Paul's understanding and outlook were being shaped, particularly after the end of World War I when he was at university, getting married and building his career. I looked for things in the works of writers of the time that might give me a window into his thinking. I read Elias Canetti's memoir *Die Fackel im Ohr* (The Torch in my Ear), about his life in the 1920s living in Leopoldstadt and courting his wife, Veza: it turned out that Haidgasse, the street where he lived, and other addresses where Veza had lived, were close to my flat in Leopoldstadt. The title of this volume of Canetti's memoirs refers to the literary and political review *Die Fackel* (The Torch) published and written by the journalist, dramatist, lecturer and social critic Karl Kraus; Kraus's lectures are a key part of the book. I gradually came to understand the important role Kraus played as a voice of conscience in Vienna, particularly during and after World War I, a war he scathingly and consistently criticised in his lectures and creative works. This was particularly so in his vast performance work *The Last Days of Mankind*, from which he would read in his lectures. Born to a Jewish family, a convert to Catholicism, and strongly critical of the role of Jewish media owners in Vienna, he represented the contradictions of assimilation in Vienna. He came to regret his conversion as he understood the threat of Nazism; his publication lost readership in the 1920s and ceased publication after his death in 1936. Paul, I think, shared Kraus's critical social perspective, but not the conflict of his conversion and its accompanying anti-Semitism. The third volume of Canetti's memoirs, *Das Augenspiel* (The Play of the Eyes), offered a rich understanding of his intellectual milieu in Vienna in the 1930s.

Canetti is one of the authors from the interwar period whom the critic Marjorie Perloff, herself a child refugee from Vienna, features in her discussion of what she calls Austro-Modernism in her book *Edge of Irony* (2016). Joseph Roth and Paul Celan, whom she also discusses, were like Canetti: Jewish, educated in German and writing in German, and from distant parts of the empire (Galicia and Bukovina, which after the collapse of the empire became incorporated into Poland, Ukraine and Romania). The end of the empire was particularly problematic for its Jewish citizens, especially for those from outside Austria. In the last fifty years under the empire, following the removal of many but not all legal and political barriers, Jews had been essentially protected in the relatively benign autocratic rule of the multicultural and multilingual empire. The nationalist reality of separate, ethnically based national states, which supplanted the empire, left no room for them. One recourse was Zionism, which of course involved abandoning Vienna and Austria altogether, and although Zionist organisations existed in Vienna and helped people leave, they never dominated Jewish institutional life there, even though Herzl, the founder of Zionism, was an assimilated Viennese Jew. This detachment from Zionism that these writers evinced was part of a general lack of faith in utopian solutions and ideologies; unlike their contemporaries in Weimar Germany, they did not have ideological commitments to Marxism and socialism, even though innovative and successful socialist policies were the hallmark of Red Vienna until 1934.

Instead, there was a deep reflection on what had been lost with the end of the Habsburg autocracy and its pluralist, supranational and multinational empire. This is particularly so in Robert Musil's *Der Mann ohne Eigenschaften* (*The Man without Qualities*), full of irony at the absurdities of the state of the empire immediately before World War I, a world that had been totally lost. Equally powerful is the wonderful *Radetzky March* by the Jewish writer Joseph Roth, a novel written after the end of the empire, reflecting with irony on its decline and fall. Roth also became a critic of the complacency of Jewish assimilation. He rediscovered his eastern empire Jewish roots in *The Wandering Jew*, an account of the lives of the remaining *Ostjuden* in the east whose compatriots had so discomfited the assimilated Viennese Jews when they began to appear in large numbers in the capital during and immediately after the war. Perloff's discussion of the vision of these writers helped me understand Paul's similar outlook. Unlike his sister, Olga, he was not a Marxist. It is notable that her socialist views would have tempered the difficulty she must have felt in returning to Vienna soon after the war. As Pat had pointed out to me, she would have found herself working with paediatricians in Vienna who had participated from 1938 in the euthanasia program for children that had been established in the beautiful Am Steinhof psychiatric hospital designed by the outstanding *Wiener Moderne* architect, Otto Wagner. Of course, she had practical reasons as well: as a paediatrician or even as a general practitioner, she was not permitted to practise by the local medical professions in either the UK or Australia. Paul, unlike Olga, found no intellectual or moral comfort in ideology after the suffering and violence he had observed and experienced, and could not live in Vienna again.

Paul's gift of Vienna to me is a forever unfolding one: both the rich interest of the city and the tragedy of its history. On each visit, I deepen my understanding, and more pleasures are discovered, as well as more troubling facts. I was delighted to find on a recent visit to Vienna an exhibition at the Museum of Applied Art of the work of Josef Hoffmann, including his furniture and design objects, as well as his buildings. I also learnt that he had embraced the Nazi regime in 1938. Such contradictions are the subject matter of the ruthless satirist of Vienna and Austria, the novelist Thomas Bernhard. In his novel *Wittgensteins Neffe* (Wittgenstein's Nephew), a mixture of memoir and fiction, Bernhard focuses on the history of Am Steinhof, as well as the hypocrisy of Vienna that awards him prizes but hates what he writes. Paul B took me to the wonderfully unrenovated Café Bräunerhof in the 1st district, which Bernhard used to frequent – there is a photo of him on the wall. We had an amusing encounter there – as we left the café, Paul B held the door open for an elderly woman in a long fur coat, who complimented him on his gentlemanly gesture, so unlike the '*amerikanische Proletariat*', she commented. 'One of the Nazi widows,' Paul explained to me after she had gone.

On my most recent visit to Vienna, I saw the recently opened Holocaust Memorial, located in a small park adjacent to the university. It consists of an oval of granite slabs, anonymous from the outside, but on the inside bearing the names and dates of the more than 65,000 Austrian Jews who were murdered in the Holocaust. It was moving to discover the names of Paul's mother, Mathilde, and Paula's best friend, Martha Müller, inscribed in the memorial. One of Brigitta Busch's young PhD students asked me what I thought: he had found the memorial a bit muted, and I was reminded of the remark by the German historian about the 'encapsulated' character of the other memorials in Vienna. I was torn; I understood what the young man meant, but I found the simplicity of the monument and the sheer volume of the names on the slabs powerful. 'They're proposing a memorial to the gay and lesbian victims of the Nazi persecution, and you can be sure that won't have a muted character,' he observed.

Chapter 3

Paul

I knew Paul when I was in my early twenties. I was too young to understand the life of this man who was nearly fifty years older, and from such a radically different world. When I started researching his life decades after his death and began to read the letters revealing his experiences and feelings after his fateful departure from Vienna, a comment in a letter to his brother-in-law Walter from June 1939 struck me: 'I have always resigned myself silently to the blows of my fate (and believe me, they were not few and not exactly gentle).' While I recognised this existential thinking from the time when I knew him, I now realised he was like this before the war, although it intensified after it, and never left him. What were these early blows, so formative of Paul's outlook on life? Who was this Paul?

As I began my research, I received an email from a total stranger, who had heard, by a chain of coincidences, that I was writing something about a Dunera Boy. It was from Dr Seumas Spark, a colleague of the late historian Ken Inglis, who had initiated an ongoing project to document, as far as possible, the lives and experiences of the Dunera Boys. 'I'm an historian at Monash. For some years I've worked on the history of the Dunera internees. I hear on the Dunera grapevine that you are writing a biography of a Dunera Boy?' In a subsequent exchange, he explained that he had learnt of my interest through a casual conversation with someone to whom I had mentioned the project – quite random, yet so fortuitous. Seumas introduced me to Elisabeth Lebensaft, a researcher who was interested in Dunera Boys who had come from Vienna. She provided some important information about Paul – about his father, his schooling and his university studies. As I pursued this further, I started to learn about the intense political and cultural history of Vienna in the years Paul spent there – an awareness of the world from which he emerged.

It began with understanding the circumstances that had brought Paul's family to Vienna, where he was born in 1901. The new freedoms of movement made possible by the granting of civil rights to the Jews of the Double Monarchy in 1867 saw many of the Jewish communities in the Habsburg Crownlands of Bohemia and Moravia shrink as their members came to Vienna to take up opportunities there. This was true of Paul's parents, both of whom were from Moravia: his mother, Mathilde, from Gross Meseritsch (today Velké Meziříčí in the Czech Republic), about 200 kilometres north of Vienna, whose Jewish population fell from around 1000 in the 1850s to around 100 within years; his father, Ignaz, from Schaffa (today Šafov in the Czech Republic), a small place about 100 kilometres northwest of Vienna. The substantial Jewish community there at that time had been involved in trading wool and woollen goods. As new trading routes bypassed Schaffa, leading to the cessation of its trading role, Paul's father moved to Vienna in 1895, aged twenty-six.

The movement of Jews to Vienna was itself a function of a broader change in the empire in the second half of the nineteenth century. The conservative Biedermeier period following the Napoleonic Wars, the period of Schubert and Metternich, of political quietism and bourgeois domesticity, was followed in the second half of the century by the *Gründerzeit*, a period of vigorous growth and industrialisation initiated after the failed liberal revolutions of 1848. The government's emphasis during this time was on modernisation, and education and greater access to opportunities based on merit. The arrival in Vienna of immigrants from all over the empire due to the rapid economic development in the period of industrialisation led to an enormous growth in population, a tripling in some sixty years. There was overcrowding, and much poverty. Most Jews who arrived settled in the 2nd district, Leopoldstadt, constituting about 30 per cent of the residents, so that it soon developed a distinctly Jewish character. The majority were Ashkenazi Jews, like Paul's parents, German speakers from Bohemia, Moravia and Hungary, secular, assimilated and increasingly indistinguishable from the general population. They differed in these respects from the increasing number of traditional Jews from the eastern fringes of the empire and beyond who were arriving in Vienna to escape poverty and, in Russia, pogroms; by 1910 they represented about a quarter of the Jewish population. These *Ostjuden* or Eastern Jews were distinctive in dress, language and religious habits, and attracted resentment and even violence.

Despite the immediate local security offered by community in Leopoldstadt, its existence was fraught with threat and instability. Widespread resentment of the enormous changes in Vienna brought about by industrialisation and immigration from the provinces fuelled anti-Semitic political movements from the 1880s, the most powerful of which was led by the immensely popular figure Karl Lueger, mayor from 1895 to 1910. Explicit anti-Semitic violence was somewhat muted in the period of growth and prosperity leading up to World

War I, and despite his rhetoric, Lueger took few directly anti-Semitic measures. Nevertheless, the rhetoric was a powder keg that could be ignited at any moment.

Paul's parents married in Vienna in 1896; their first child, Paul's sister, Olga, was born in 1898; Paul was born three years later, just after the turn of the century. Paul's father ran a grocery store in Leopoldstadt, at Novaragasse 37; the family lived in a modest apartment next door at Novaragasse 39. Novaragasse was a narrow street of apartment buildings housing relocated families like the Kurzes; there were some shops on the ground floor. The Riesenrad, the giant Ferris wheel that has remained an iconic symbol of Vienna ever since it was erected in 1897 to celebrate the Golden Jubilee of Emperor Franz Josef, was the outstanding feature of the amusement park of the nearby Prater, a much larger park and leisure ground, which had once been the emperor's hunting ground.

Life in Leopoldstadt before the outbreak of World War I was vibrant, dynamic and troubled. Paul's early life was surrounded by a broader potential for disruption and the threat of violence. His secondary education was conducted during a period of the most chaotic and revolutionary change. In 1911, when Paul first enrolled in the eight-year course of study leading to the university entrance examination, the Matura, Emperor Franz Joseph was eighty-one; he had been emperor for over sixty years. The city of Vienna had celebrated his diamond jubilee in 1908 in grand style, with 12,000 of the Kaiser's subjects from all parts of the empire parading along the Ringstrasse. By the time of Paul's matriculation in 1919, World War I had caused enormous hardship in Vienna, the empire had collapsed in the aftermath of its catastrophic military defeat, and social revolution was underway.

The name, location and character of the high school that Paul attended from the age of ten, the *Sperlgymnasium*, on Kleine Sperlgasse, were emblematic of these vast changes in the last decades of the empire that were the larger context for Paul's early life. The school's name reflected the area's changing character. It turned out that prior to 1877 the site had been occupied by an iconic Biedermeier building, Zum Sperl, the most famous dance hall of the time, for which the composer of the famous 'Radetzky March', Johann Strauss Sr, had composed dance music, including several named for it: the 'Sperl Festwalzer', the 'Sperl Gallop' and the 'Sperl Polka'. In 1908, only three years before Paul was enrolled, the *Sperl* had been converted to a *Realgymnasium*, reflecting the recent educational reform designed to meet the needs of the rapidly industrialising empire. A *Realgymnasium* differed from the traditional *Gymnasium* in placing a greater emphasis on science (biology, physics and chemistry); it taught modern languages in place of classical Greek.

The *Sperlgymnasium* had several famous alumni from Jewish families like Paul's who had moved to Vienna: Freud attended the school from 1865, shortly after its founding (it had originally been located in a smaller building nearby), and other Jewish alumni a generation younger than Paul included Freud's younger colleague Alfred Adler, the composer Arnold Schönberg, and the health reformer of Red Vienna Julius Tandler. The founder of logotherapy, Viktor Frankl, attended five years after Paul. The education such schools offered was demanding. Only about 2 per cent of Austrian school students attended a *Gymnasium* of any kind, and of these only roughly a quarter successfully completed the Matura.

I traced the route from Paul's home to the school: it was a ten-minute walk from Novaragasse, along Zirkusgasse and past the Karmeliterkirche (Carmelite Church), the school building lying diagonally opposite the church and its square. In the years Paul was at the school, three-quarters of the over 500 students, almost all of them boys, were Jewish.

Paul's parents must have strongly encouraged academic achievement and professional ambition: Paul and Olga each passed the Matura, attended university and obtained a professional academic degree (Olga became a paediatrician, Paul a chemical engineer). This was rather unusual for such first-generation immigrant families, according to Elisabeth Lebensaft.

Within three years of Paul starting at the *Realgymnasium*, World War I had started. In July 1914 the acerbic social critic Karl Kraus, in the immediate aftermath of the assassination of the Archduke Franz Ferdinand, the heir to the throne, in Sarajevo, had made the prophetic remark that Austria was the 'research laboratory for world destruction'. A particular risk to Paul's family was the chronic food shortages in Vienna: the fact that Paul's father was a grocer meant that not only was he affected by the insecurity of supply, but he was also vulnerable to the frustrations of consumers. The poor harvest of 1914, the loss of the grain-growing areas of Eastern Galicia to the Russian advance and the decision of Hungary to prioritise local demand led to rationing from 1914, and endless queuing for food, often overnight and without success. The food situation became more acute during the war; it was far worse in Vienna than in Berlin, Paris or London. Already by August 1916 thousands were lining up for fat and butter.

I came across a University of Vienna study of the police reports of the war years, which gave me a powerful glimpse of the atmosphere Paul's father's business faced:

> At 2 o'clock in the morning, about 3000 people lined up for flour in front of the Wagner company in the 2nd district (Leopoldstadt). Supplies were exhausted by midday, with two thirds of those queuing going away empty-handed. Despite the sellout, the

unsatisfied waited another four hours in front of the store ... The people waiting in the markets and in front of the stores were by no means peaceful. Again and again there were quarrels between those lined up, and damage to property. The targets of the anger of the queuing people were also the guards, who were not only insulted by the waiting crowd, but also spat at. In some cases the guards had so much trouble in bringing order among the excited queues that stores had to be closed at short notice.

Shop owners were among those seen as responsible by frustrated residents, who accused them of price gouging, holding back supplies and giving preferential treatment to those who could pay more. Once the crowds were upset, the situation could also quickly escalate, against the guard, the store owners or sellers. Shop owners became the object of government rules and constraints, echoing the public mood. Food supply became centralised, as without centralisation, the authorities argued, many small businessmen looked after their regular customers and traded goods between themselves and, therefore, many goods were not available to the public. There were ongoing threats to business for these shopkeepers:

> Continued lack of fat, bread and flour increased the already existing exasperation and it seemed that the outbreak of major demonstrations and extraordinary rumours circulated by unknown parties were causing panic. On August 1 [1917], there was talk of a general strike as a peace demonstration, of the looting of department stores and stores, and the introduction of breadless days ... many anxious businessmen announced their intention to keep their stores and market stalls closed on that day.

Hunger marches to the town hall from outlying districts passed along Taborstrasse, at the other end of Novaragasse, where they were dispersed by guards.

*

As the war proceeded, and the Crown Lands to the east were occupied by the Czarist army, more traditional Jewish communities were forced to leave and arrived in numbers in Vienna, particularly in Leopoldstadt. Their presence had become a focus for anti-Semitism from the very beginning of the war, intensifying as food shortages worsened and the lack of success in the war became more and more apparent. Mass anti-Semitic demonstrations began in June 1918 (continuing on a larger scale, and sometimes violently, until 1923), Jews, particularly *Ostjuden*, being blamed for shortages of food, housing and fuel. I found a police report from June 1917 that gave an indication of the dangerous atmosphere:

> The mood of the demonstrators was desperate, as people could not buy anything at the markets, which were almost completely devoid of food. There were threats of demolition and looting … Criticism was again directed against the authorities and the government. They were accused of doing nothing for the people and simply leaving them to starve. It allegedly only cared about the high-ranking officials and Jews. In contrast to the other strata of the population, the rich would live as before the war. One would never see them queuing.

In January 1918 there was a general strike. The crucial final year of Paul's education, 1918–19, as he prepared for the Matura examination, was particularly turbulent. In September 1918, just as the school year was starting, his studies were interrupted by the arrival in Vienna of the Spanish Influenza epidemic. Schools were closed the following month, when mortality reached its peak. What happened next helped to make sense of something Paul had told me once, noting its irony: that he had fought for the Kaiser on the Italian front in World War I. He joined the army. Perhaps this was an opportunity to fulfill the general Austrian obligation of two- or three-years' military service, which in turn was a requirement for entry to the University of Vienna. Paul turned seventeen in September 1918, meaning that he was eligible to volunteer for the army (eligibility for conscription was eighteen). Although Paul had not yet graduated, a graduate of the *Gymnasium* had the privilege of one-year, volunteer service as an officer candidate followed by a year in the reserve. But the Imperial and Royal Army was falling apart: there were mass desertions, and released prisoners from the Russian front were forced into combat units again, which they deeply resented. The Italian front was in the foothills of the Alps, in the Veneto region; a final push by the Italian forces in October led to a massive defeat of the Austrians, and it was clear the war was about to end soon. The influenza pandemic was wreaking havoc among the troops. It was a strange time indeed to be volunteering, but it seems that Paul did, as did others of his age cohort. Efforts to find archival records of his service have been fruitless, although according to Elisabeth Lebensaft, this is not unusual, given that he would have served for a few weeks only in the dying days of the war and amid the chaos on the Italian front as the old monarchy collapsed. Ironically, the treaty that stated the terms on which the war was ended abolished conscription, so the need to get his military service out of the way was unnecessary.

After demobilisation at the conclusion of the war in November 1918, Paul returned to school for his final year of studies. It was not an easy time to be preparing for the Matura examination, which was to be held in late spring of the following year. The atmosphere in Vienna was chaotic. Hundreds of thousands of discharged soldiers were returning to Vienna or transiting through, and there was a revolutionary atmosphere as Emperor Karl abdicated and the empire collapsed. The nations of the empire declared independence; Austria remained a relatively small German-speaking rump of the empire. Soldiers' and workers' councils, on the Soviet model, were formed. The Socialist forces were split, some advocating a revolution, on the model of Russia and Germany, others committing themselves to democratic means. The split was dramatically illustrated in the Adler family. Adler *père*, Victor, the leader of the socialists, was a moderate; Adler *fils*, Friedrich (Fritz) was a radical, who in 1916 in protest of the war assassinated the then prime minister as he was dining. Adler was convicted and sentenced but was released by Emperor Karl shortly before the end of the war, having become a central voice in opposition to the war, which was now widespread. The Red Guard, a small revolutionary group, including the journalist Egon Erwin Kisch, who became notorious after a visit to Australia in 1934, where he hastily attempted a sudden, bungled attempt at an attack on the parliament at its opening in November 1918. There was great anxiety about the security situation in Vienna with the return of so many hungry and embittered soldiers. Armed militias formed with the support of the government for a few months, including, extraordinarily, a Jewish one, whose main task was guarding the bridges leading into Leopoldstadt and preventing anti-Semitic attacks, a persistent threat. These militias were absorbed into the new regular army within a few months.

With extraordinary determination in these tumultuous circumstances, Paul successfully completed the Matura in 1919 and entered the Technische Hochschule (the present-day Technical University Vienna) to study chemical engineering, a four-year degree. The university was prestigious, having been founded over a century earlier and occupying a prominent building located centrally in Karlsplatz, near the famous Karlskirche.

I wondered what Paul's life was like as a student here. As before, useful leads suddenly appeared. I found a volume produced to mark the 200th anniversary of the founding of the university, written in German and English, focusing precisely on the period 1914–37. Parts of it were available to read online, but the most relevant sections were not. Improbably, a copy of the volume was held by my university library. I called the archives department of the Technical University, who gave me a quick and helpful response on the details of Paul's studies there. But then a further small miracle: the archivist explained that the university was in the process of investigating Paul's life and fate, part of a project to trace what had happened to its Jewish students and teachers, initially those who were expelled in 1938, but subsequently any of its former students who had suffered persecution. Paul's name was already on their list to follow up. From these resources I gained a window into Paul's life as a student in those difficult, violent years following the end of World War I and the dissolution of the empire.

Paul entered the Technische Hochschule in autumn 1919 at a time of continuing turmoil in Vienna, a year of dire shortages and social disturbances. The economic and general living situation in the immediate aftermath of the war was even worse than that during the war. Coal supplies for the winter were non-existent, and people were starving. The facilities at the university were stretched to the limit: resources, heating and equipment were inadequate. Students competed for laboratory access, textbooks and even food in the student dining hall; many were in poverty, as the value of whatever scholarships were on offer was entirely wiped out by the period of inflation and hyperinflation from 1919 until 1921. Demobilisation meant that the size of the student cohort was significantly increased, putting further pressure on resources. The composition of the student body reflected the social and political conditions. About 20 per cent of the students were 'foreign'; that is, not ordinarily resident in the rump state that was left of the former empire. They were from the former eastern parts of the empire, now the independent states of Czechoslovakia, Hungary, Ukraine and Poland, where, if they were Jewish, they were often subjected to quotas or outright exclusion. Around 20 per cent of the students in the university overall were Jewish. There were only a handful of women, either as students, admitted for the first time in 1919, or staff. What few women there were tended to gravitate to Paul's discipline, chemistry, rather than to the other larger and more central disciplines of civil, mechanical and electrical engineering. This was partly because the smaller size of the chemistry program was more attractive to women, and partly because chemical engineers could get a position in industrial laboratories, where women had demonstrated their capacities during the war years. There were occasional and usually temporary female members of staff, mostly working as chemistry assistants.

Paul certainly directly experienced the anti-Semitism that had intensified in the closing years of the war, and which threatened the Jewish students on campus during his time there. The conservative German nationalist student associations at Austrian universities had a long tradition of excluding Jewish students, and this became more politicised during the latter years of the war and in the immediate postwar years. While Jewish and socialist students had their own clubs, they were excluded from representation on the student body recognised by the university, which consisted exclusively of German nationalist students. There were demonstrations and violence between different student groups, by 1923 culminating in attacks by nationalist and overtly Nazi students, who beat up Jewish and socialist students both on campus and off, in some cases dragging them out of lectures to do so. The German nationalist students lobbied from 1919 for the imposition of a quota for Jewish students of 10 per cent; the proposal was supported by the Council of Professors in 1923. The professoriate had its own policies of exclusion: the appointment of a Jewish professor in 1920 was quickly rescinded; the appointment of a Jewish historian as the rector of Prague University in 1922 led to a student strike and the temporary closure of the universities in Vienna. By 1938, when Jews were excluded from university posts after the Anschluss, few posts were vacated at the Technische Hochschule. In the Republican era (1918–33/38), only one Jewish professor, Emil Abel, was appointed at the university. Paul attended his course *Physikalische Chemie* in his first year.

Despite these extraordinarily difficult conditions, Paul graduated in 1923 with an engineering degree and the prestigious title of *Ingenieur*, restricted to such graduates from 1917. But the social and political circumstances meant that he had graduated with an understanding of a great deal more than his specialty: how thin the veneer of civilisation could be, and what potential for violence lay underneath, waiting to emerge. Paul saw human oppression, of which he was consistently aware, as not something that could be solved by ideological means. Yet his vision of life was tragic not nihilistic: he remained deeply committed to critical understanding, and to scientific progress. His warmth and desire to educate us in human understanding was anything but cynical.

I have no details of Paul's life after he entered the workforce in 1923. The political and cultural context of this period was marked by ongoing turbulence and threat. Postwar inflation and hyperinflation had, by 1922, wiped out people's savings, and the new republic was on the point of bankruptcy, from which it was only rescued by an international loans agreement and the creation of a new currency. From 1922 until 1929, the economy gradually improved until it again collapsed following the Wall Street Crash. Politically, the federal government, led in the immediate postwar period by the Social Democrats, was replaced within a year by a conservative Christian Social administration, which ruled until the abolition of democracy in 1934.

Vienna, which now constituted a province and hence was relatively independent, remained firmly in the hands of the Social Democrats, who embarked on a successful program of social housing, healthcare, sanitation and educational reform – the period known as 'Red Vienna'. I visited exhibitions and explored areas of the city notable for the achievements of Red Vienna, once with Brigitta and Thomas. Writers of this period, such as Sperber and Canetti, testify to the richness and creativity of their lives in Vienna at the time, despite the difficulty of the economic and political conditions.

The fragility of the political structures in postwar Austria was underlined by the creation of independent militias by the social democratic and conservative Catholic forces, which clashed in demonstrations, sometimes violently. In one such clash in a provincial town, an adult and a child were killed by members of the conservative militia; they were charged but acquitted in a jury trial on 15 July 1927. The Social Democrats called for demonstrations in Vienna in protest, but these turned into a riot as the crowd marched on the Ringstrasse, at first attempting unsuccessfully to attack the university building, then parliament, and finally the Palace of Justice, which they succeeded in setting on fire. The police response to this act led to the death of eighty-nine protestors by gunfire. The Viennese philosopher Karl Popper, who was twenty-four at the time, wrote, 'I began to expect the worst: that the democratic bastions of Central Europe would fall, and that a totalitarian Germany would start another war.' The violence led Elias Canetti to write his profound work on the psychology of crowds, *Crowds and Power*.

The economic collapse during the Great Depression led to further social and political conflict, including a constitutional crisis involving the indefinite suspension of parliament in 1933 and ongoing battles between the militias, culminating in a brief civil war in February 1934 involving the federal armed forces, in which the Social Democrats were defeated. The civil war saw an assault on the *Gemeindebauten* (social housing), one of the distinctive achievements of the Social Democratic government of Vienna, particularly the Karl Marx Hof, which had been fortified as it was being built in anticipation of such an attack. The civil war spelled the end of democracy; a new constitution installed an authoritarian form of single-party government known as Austro-Fascism. The conservative forces forming the government were closely allied to the Catholic Church; they were thus strenuously opposed to the anti-clerical policies of the Nazis, who were growing in influence following their rise to power in Germany in 1933. Shortly after the civil war, in July 1934, a Nazi putsch, in which Chancellor Engelbert Dollfuss was murdered, was quickly defeated. Dollfuss's successor as chancellor, Kurt Schuschnigg, continued to assert Austrian independence from the Nazi state; his government even gained support from liberal quarters as the only bulwark against Nazism. In February 1938, Schuschnigg's negotiations with Hitler to secure Austrian independence failed, and the resulting Anschluss, or unification with the Third Reich, occurred to massive popular support days afterwards. The new Nazi regime immediately implemented humiliating and violent measures against the Jewish population.

Despite these chaotic times Paul managed to work. From February 1930, he was employed by Hofmann und Czerny, a piano manufacturer, which had a huge factory in Vienna in the 13th district. It was the largest piano manufacturer on the continent. Paul became the operations manager. Now secure in his employment, in March 1932 he and Paula married. It was a minimal ceremony; neither set of parents were present, only Olga and Walter, as witnesses. The new couple moved into an apartment in Vienna's 6th district, sharing it with an aunt on Paul's side, Grete Willheim, an unmarried opera singer who was only a little older than they were. Three years after the wedding, in April 1935, a catastrophe – Paul's father, Ignaz, died by suicide, hanging himself in the family apartment in Novaragasse. In our interactions with him, Paul never referred to it, and avoided any mention of his father, so the circumstances of his suicide remain obscure – was it a result of financial difficulty? Or other political or emotional factors? And then, in March 1938, the Anschluss: by the end of June, Paul had been removed from his position as operations manager at Hoffmann und Czerny. The search for an exit from Vienna was to begin.

*

I had come to understand something of the blows of fate that had shaped Paul's outlook on life. I was better able to understand his expression: 'After all, we are nothing more than a little ball of feathers that is pushed around, dented, shattered, straightened up, blown up, puffed up by someone or something to happiness or unhappiness.'

I remember a moment in London, three years after I had moved there, when my flatmate told me the news that Paul had died – Pat had written to us. It was as if I had been hit in the solar plexus; I was totally unprepared for the impact. I was twenty-seven. Now, in my seventies, I feel his nurturing presence more intensely than ever, and have come to understand him and his life better through his wartime letters and through archives and published material about the times in which he lived. There is something else I cherish: a postcard and a letter from him that I still have.

First the postcard. This was from when Paul had come to London while I was there, en route to Olga in Vienna. He had wanted to show me the actual Staatsoper as part of my education. But as second best he had taken me to see Bizet's *Carmen* at the Royal Opera House, my first time at the opera. 'The human voice is a musical instrument, infinitely more flexible than a mechanical instrument,' he explained. When he got to Olga's, he sent me a card of the grand main staircase of the Vienna opera: 'Main Staircase. Operas in Vienna mean and meant quite something different to London. Obviously. This could supply a philosophical literary ethnological thesis.'

The letter is full of such philosophical reflections, based on vast reading experience. 'Words can be a very tricky way of communication and the legal language, especially the Corpus Juris Civilis of the Roman Empire, tried, emphasis is on "tried", to evade these tricks. To my humble perception, unsuccessfully.' I had written about what I felt was the 'irresponsibility' of the recently elected Labour government. Paul responded:

The word "irresponsibility" is not applicable. The word to be used is "naïveté". A baby is neither responsible nor irresponsible, nor is it naïve or a-naïve, it is on the road of learning. Naïveté in men who are already past the stage of learning means, that they failed to learn, to perceive, to gauge, to coordinate, in short to have a horizon. Singularly they can be quite amicable men. I'm quite sure that Dr Cairns [a leading member of the Labour government] is a nice idealistic guy. But I wonder whether he has ever experienced a brainwashed mob of any sort and if so, whether he has the ability to perceive such a mob. But all that is old thrash and silly to write about. Politicians have to be naïve.

'A brainwashed mob' – Paul had such experiences: the days after the Anschluss, the pogroms on Kristallnacht, and earlier, the mob burning down the Palace of Justice in 1927.

I had been reading books about economics and finance for my work in London, as I was teaching Business English to specialists in finance, and realised how absolutely little I knew. Here he responded with a reminder of how complex it was to understand human social organisation and the danger of eliminating sources of understanding, which he saw in Marxism:

Yes, Tim, economics. Not that I know much of it, I only know about it. A most fascinating faculty. Embraces a dozen subjects (geology, geography, climatology, social structures, politics general and singular, law, banking, finance, statistics, mathematics [gambling]). I am proud of you that you started to see that nothing is simple. I often wonder, whereto are certain abilities of the human brain of certain types of homo sapiens shifted when, like in the case of economics, most branches of that faculty are crudely killed in totalitarian states.

I must have referred to my Celtic origins: 'Your barbaric ancestors, the Celts. Vienna. Yes, in one of the many museums in Vienna there are plenty of artefacts of Celtic make archeologically excavated in the Viennese basin. Celts belong to the Indo Germanic group of races. Jews belong to the Semitic. This is a statement only. If you start thinking phantasy about it, that is your business. Do not blame me for it or the Celts.' It was only years later that I understood what he was referring to – the basis of Nazi race theory in nineteenth-century philology and anthropology. His mordant humour showed: 'I did not know that man can live without a spleen. OK, but I could not live without spleen-fulness.' He listened to a series of talks by Ralf Dahrendorf, the head of the London School of Economics. 'It is a very, very long time that I have heard such a rational human talk. And he is German. Yes, there are even Jews who are not Shylocks.'

Such a distinctive voice, so intelligent and alive. Such a fortuitous collision of fates, that the featherball of Paul's fate had brought him and his deep humanity on the *Dunera* to Australia, and into our lives.

Part 2
Paul and Paula

This is a story about a separation, imposed by violence. A separation whose outcome remained fearfully, despairingly uncertain.

Paula and Paul, early 1930s

It is time to tell the story of Paul and Paula from the moment of their separation in 1939. I have tried to present it strictly factually, using the material of the letters, bringing the disparate sources of evidence about events and feelings together to make a sequential narrative. There are many stories of experiences of Viennese Jews at the time of the Holocaust, but fewer from original sources, and I have let the sources speak for themselves. I have assembled the facts of the story in honour of Paul, and I dedicate it to his memory.

Kurz family in 1939

Ignaz Kurz 1869–1935 (Paul's father, deceased)

Mathilde (Paul's mother, 64yo, b. 1875)

    Olga Kurz (Paul's sister, 41yo, b. 1898)

    Paul Kurz (38yo, b. 1901), married to Paula Haim

Haim family in 1939

'Omama' (Paula's grandmother, 80yo, b. 1859)

    Martin Haim (Paula's father, 80yo, b. 1859)

    Antonie ('Tonie') (Paula's mother, 70yo, b. 1869)

        Hans Haim (Paula's brother, 50yo, b. 1889), married to Lisl

        Alice Haim (Paula's sister, 48yo, b. 1891)

        Paula Haim (43yo, b. 1896), married to Paul Kurz

        Walter ('Bobbi') Haim (Paula's brother, 37yo, b. 1902), married to Lilly (20yo, b. 1919)

Chapter 1

Leaving Vienna
April 1939

After months of effort and endless bureaucratic delay, Paul Kurz had finally managed to get a passport and a visitor's visa for England to join his sister, Olga. As a Jew, Paul had lost his right to work in November 1938 as the restrictions imposed on Jews in the former Austria following the Anschluss inexorably rolled out. Olga, a paediatrician, had gone to England as a domestic servant in 1938. Paul would join her and use the time in England to prepare for his family's permanent exile from Vienna. His wife, Paula, had the right to go with him, but in the end decided to stay in Vienna for the time being with her ageing parents and Paul's mother. She was aware of the risk of this delay. On 25 April 1939, the evening of Paul's departure, she wrote to her younger brother, Walter, who had made it to New York in February 1939, waiting to be joined by his young fiancée, Lilly: 'Today was a difficult day for us. Paul flew to London at 3:30 in the afternoon. And I sit here and do not know whether I have destroyed my life because I remained here. Time will tell.'

Time would, indeed, tell.

Paula was the third of four siblings, Paul the younger of two. They had married one Thursday afternoon in March 1932: he was thirty, living with his parents; she was thirty-five, living with her parents and her older unmarried sister, Alice, in the old family home, an apartment on Margaretenstrasse, in the 5th district. The wedding was a starkly minimalist, private affair, held in a synagogue neither near Paul's family home in Novaragasse in the 2nd district, Leopoldstadt, nor near Paula's family home, but in the Stadttempel in the 1st district. There was only the minimum attendance – two witnesses: Walter and Olga, who was also a close friend to Paula. It was highly unusual for a female, Olga, to act as a formal witness to the wedding. Neither Paul's nor Paula's parents attended, nor the other members of Paula's family. The austere occasion suited Paul's serious temperament: for him, marriage was a private thing, not a cause for public celebration.

Paul had studied chemical engineering in the years immediately following World War I. This was a time of great social and economic hardship, and was accompanied by an upsurge of anti-Semitic violence, particularly on university campuses. Despite the difficult social, political and economic conditions in Vienna through much of the 1920s and 1930s, Paul had made a success of his career: by the time all Jewish employees were dismissed in November 1938, Paul was working as a plant manager in a large company that manufactured pianos, 'dictator of 500 workers', as he ruefully wrote later. Paula had worked as a bookkeeper and auditor in her father's accounting firm. Up until two months before Paul's departure, the couple were sharing a fashionable apartment with Grete, technically an aunt of Paul's, though close to him in age. The apartment was in a strikingly beautiful building, the Litoralishof, a Jugendstil (Art Nouveau) building on the Linke

Wienzeile in the 6th district, not far from the famous public food market, the Naschmarkt.

Paula had only two really close friends: 'I have always considered this title [friend] sacred and don't grant it so easily,' she wrote to Walter. One was Olga, roughly the same age as she. The depth of her feeling for Olga is shown in a remark in a letter to Walter two years after Olga's departure and sixteen months after Paul's. She is starved of news of them, for which she is dependent on Walter in New York: 'You know that I depend on these two with each beat of my heart.' Her other friend was a younger woman, Martha Müller, and like Olga a paediatrician: Olga had been Martha's direct superior and had come to value her strength and loyalty. Martha and Paula had presumably met and become friends through Olga, or perhaps she had met Olga through Martha. After Olga's departure from Vienna in August 1938, Martha was the closest of all Paula's acquaintances there.

Paul's departure was part of a steady exodus of family and friends. 'Here friends and acquaintances emigrate daily and hourly, including many to the US. You become a rarity here,' Paula's older brother, Hans, a businessman, wrote to Walter, shortly after Paul's departure. The extent of the violent hostility towards Jews among the general population, and its political manifestation, had become frighteningly clear in the previous year. The eve of the Anschluss on 12 March 1938 had seen pogrom-style riots in Vienna, and the arriving German troops and the Nazi leadership were received rapturously. Hitler's address in the Heldenplatz, part of the Imperial Palace grounds, three days later was attended by tens of thousands of cheering supporters. The new regime exerted relentless pressure on Jews to leave: severe restrictions were introduced on the capacity of Jews to work, to run businesses and to move freely around the city. Adolf Eichmann established the

Central Agency for Jewish Emigration in Vienna in August 1938, which became a model for the systematic expulsion and dispossession of the Jewish population in other parts of the Reich. In the pogrom of 9–10 November 1938, Kristallnacht, of Vienna's ninety-three Jewish institutional buildings (synagogues and prayer houses) only one, the Stadttempel in the 1st district, where Paul and Paula had been married, was spared from destruction, and only because of fears that the flames would spread to adjoining, non-Jewish buildings. The extent of violence in Vienna on Kristallnacht was greater than in any other city of the Reich; the Nazi authorities had to rein in the mobs. Paula's family was directly affected. Hans was arrested but released the same day through the intervention of a sympathetic friend. Walter's future father-in-law was held in prison in Vienna for two months from that date.

The violence and arrests sharply increased the pressure on the victims to find a way out. Paul, Paula and family joined the tens of thousands of Jewish people looking to leave Austria, now incorporated into the German Reich. The process of seeking an exit from Vienna for a safe refuge abroad was bewildering and exhausting, even while Jews were still allowed, even encouraged, to leave (having been first stripped of all their assets and subsequently their nationality). There were heavily restrictive quotas on entry for Jews to other countries. Countries attending the notorious Évian conference in July 1938 on the plight of the hundreds of thousands of stateless Jews from Germany and the former Austria failed, with one or two notable exceptions, to make commitments to receiving the refugees, handing a propaganda victory to Hitler. Australia's chief delegate, Colonel T.W. White, had declared: 'As we have no real racial problem [sic], we are not desirous of importing one by encouraging any scheme of large-scale foreign migration.'

The United States, a favoured destination for refugees, had a limited annual quota, which scarcely changed following the Évian meeting, a painful irony given that the US had instigated it. The process of applying to the US was extraordinarily complicated: as Hans put it to Walter, 'You know best through your own experience how the local American consulate draws out everything with regard to affidavits, and other than affidavits still other formalities and confirmations (bank identifications, notary confirmations and I don't know what).' No fewer than thirteen separate documents, in multiple copies, often notarised, were required for a complete application. The process was made immeasurably more difficult by the stringent and bureaucratic requirements of, and humiliating procedures put in place by, the Nazi authorities for obtaining a passport, which involved declaration of assets, tax status and payment of exorbitant taxes and fines; the departing individual could take few or no assets.

Applications for the United States, once received, were assessed locally. Those registered as intending immigrants to the US were allocated a numerical position in the quota queue: an annual quota of 27,370 existed for people born in Germany and Austria (the quotas were combined in 1938 following the Anschluss), vastly fewer than the number seeking admission. An excruciating process of waiting followed; those who had not registered early enough and were further down the queue, evident by their high number, knew they had little chance of success but still desperately hung on in case some miracle should happen. In July 1938, when they registered, Paul and Paula were given the registration numbers 36,776 and 36,777 respectively; these were registration numbers for Vienna alone, just one of many cities in the Reich in which people were applying. This was the only year in which America's German quota was filled. And exactly at this time, the US tightened up and slowed down its approval process, so the 1939 quota was not filled.

One key requirement of this assessment was the affidavit of support – a financial guarantee from the guarantor on the US side. This was assessed in relation to the guarantor's financial situation, their relation to the applicant, their motivation to act as guarantor and the number of other applicants they were sponsoring. Although Paul and Paula had completed initial registration for emigration, they lacked these affidavits. Neither of them had relatives in the US who could act as guarantors (Walter, who had only just arrived, had insecure employment and very limited financial resources). Affidavits had to come from individuals, not community or religious organisations, and involved personal commitments and financial disclosures. Paul and Paula were, therefore, in the difficult position of trying to get strangers to act in this capacity. One potential avenue was Hans, who was treasurer of the Sephardic community organisation in Vienna. The family on the father's side was originally from Turkey, Paula's paternal grandfather settling in Vienna in the 1840s, his wife's family having settled there two decades earlier. Hans communicated with the Sephardic organisations in New York about sponsorship affidavits, and in April, a number of affidavits for members of the Viennese Sephardic community were received; Hans encouraged Walter to press the case for affidavits for Paul and Paula in person through local community contacts in New York. Paul also appealed to him. This was a demanding task for Walter, who was reticent and lacking in confidence, not really cut out for this role.

Paul's preferred destination for emigration was not the US, where Walter now was, but Australia. Paul's career as a chemical engineer was a factor in deciding on potential places of exile. During World

War I, the lab of one of the chemistry professors, Hugo Strache, at the university where Paul had studied, had worked on the extraction and large-scale production of fatty acids and soaps (fatty acids were used in ammunition production). Perhaps influenced by this teacher, and the tradition of the wool trade in Schaffa, his father's hometown in Moravia, Paul became an expert in the production of lanolin from wool grease. Lanolin had only been named in 1882 by the noted Jewish chemist Oskar Liebreich: the patent was bought by Benno Jaffé, also Jewish, who produced it in what became the Pfeilring Werke in Berlin. Paul's work at the piano manufacturer, Hofmann und Czerny, involved lanolin, as the hammers in pianos that struck the strings crucially had a pad of wool felt, the quality of which directly affected the quality of the sound. 'I am a chemist not only through studies but also in my soul,' Paul wrote. He was proud of his skills: 'Hardly 100 chemists in the whole world have mastered this area as well as I,' he claimed.

As for the United States, it was 'absolutely not the land of my dreams,' he wrote. Instead, Paul dreamed of reuniting the whole family in Sydney, where Martha Müller's sister had managed to relocate; Martha and her mother were to follow. 'Family Müller are already prepared in every respect to leave soon for Australia,' he wrote to Martha's brother-in-law in Sydney, who was helping him. He was trying to get in touch with firms involved in lanolin production there, one of which was building a new factory. His initial contact with the Australian immigration authorities in early 1939 was discouraging, as his application was rejected. Yet perhaps his Müller contacts in Sydney would be able to advance his cause with the local Jewish agencies. 'Tell them please that we are known to you as very clever, skilful and painstaking people who are only missing influential connexions in the world and that we are willing to accept any position that might be offered to us,' he wrote to them. Perhaps, too, something could be found for Olga to enable her to work, and even a possible guarantor for his mother. Paul was not entirely opposed to the United States, of course, if that could be a safe haven; the main thing was to reunite the family, including Paula, Olga and their parents.

Paul envisaged going to England as an opportunity for him to get an Australian visa there, which he thought would take a couple of months. In the meantime, he would seek work in his profession; England had a well-established wool industry, centred on Bradford. This would allow Paula to join him later on. Another crucial consideration was that by going to England he and Paula would be joining Olga, who was isolated there. Olga's departure from Vienna in August of the previous year was timely, as a month later all Jewish doctors in Vienna were removed from their posts. Yet Olga could not work as a doctor in England either: the local medical profession made it impossible for émigré doctors to practise there, a policy mirrored in Australia. Instead, she was working as a domestic servant for Mr and Mrs Humphris and their three children (a three-year-old, Danny, and newborn twins) on a farm in Kidderminster, near Birmingham, in the Midlands. (UK work visas for domestic servants, mostly female, were readily available.) Initially, on arrival in England, Paul would join her there and work for the family in exchange for food and board, 'a degreed house servant who eats the bread of charity', in his own words, while he sought professional work. Several months earlier, Paula had written to Mrs Humphris suggesting a similar arrangement for herself, and sent a soft toy for Danny, then two; in February Mrs Humphris replied, offering Paula a job as a cook.

When Paul's visitor's visa suddenly came through, Paula found herself not yet ready to leave. The letter granting the entry visa for Paul arrived on 1 February 1939, as the family was recovering emotionally from Walter's departure for America only the previous day. 'This morning we received a permit for Paul and his wife,' Paula wrote. 'That would be me! Funny! I hadn't dreamt of leaving yet.' The wording in the formal letter from the British Consulate required her to adopt an identity constructed for her, not one that she could easily embrace: a life as 'wife' in an English-speaking environment. And which one? She and Paul had not been able to agree. Paul's goal was Australia: he would go on ahead, and then bring the family. Olga supported this idea. For Paula, the thought of distant Australia was alarming: 'How terrible that is for me you can imagine,' she wrote. 'I have always known that for me it would end at the farthest place on earth.' For Paula, America, where her brother now was, or England, if Paul could get work there, was preferable. And another important factor was the situation of the parents – Paula's parents Martin, eighty, and Tonie, seventy, and Paul's mother, Mathilde, now sixty-four, for whom it was virtually impossible to arrange visas, given their age. 'The old problem of what one will do with the old people remains crushingly hopeless,' Paul wrote. The impossibility of the choices facing them, and possibly Paula's ambivalence, were intensely stressful; he began to lose weight. The irony of the consternation caused by the news of the visa was not lost on Paula: 'We really don't deserve getting something like this. Anyone else would be beaming.' A compromise was reached within a couple of weeks: Paul would go on alone, and Paula would follow later.

> *We expect that Paul will go soon to England for a couple of months to keep working on the correspondence to Australia, then travel there alone and we then can all join him. (When will that be? When the Messiah comes?) But perhaps there will be a position available for him*

somewhere in England, so that he can exchange his visitor's visa for a work visa. In that case I would soon go as a cook or something like that, or some sort of servant and so be able to look after the old people. Then we would all be in England until we would all be allowed to join you in New York.

'One must begin, the others will soon follow', was Paul's attitude; there would then be a race to see who could reunite the family first, he (in Australia) or Walter (in New York). In March, there was encouraging news from Australia: a Jewish agency had found a local financial guarantor for Paul and his wife. 'A guarantor has turned up,' she wrote to Walter, 'and so a permit for us is as good as certain. Perhaps it is not so bad. It is certainly easier there than in the USA and you can certainly come there then. And everyone, everyone else too!' Moreover, Paula was fully aware of the risk of her decision: 'I will provisionally remain here. We don't need to go together, "two by two". It was certainly easier for him, but I won't do it because of all the parents. We can only hope that we (Paul and I) will be able to meet again.' The risk and uncertainty were killing them: 'I am afraid. Terribly,' wrote Paula.

Paul's preparations to leave for England coincided with them moving out of their smart flat in Litoralishof in early February and back into Paula's parents' apartment in Margaretenstrasse; this meant giving up their fashionable furniture – something that seemed of little consequence to Paula, in comparison with her brother's absence and Paul's imminent departure. However, it took nearly three months for Paul to get all his papers in order so that he could leave, time that could hardly be afforded, given how limited it was for them to resolve their situation. His papers were lost in the tax office, delaying the granting of a passport, which then had to be lodged with the British

Consulate, where it was again delayed. Finally, Paul's passport was returned with the visa in mid-April and he was free to leave a week later. Obtaining a German passport and exit visa meant the (Jewish) applicant was obligated to leave Greater Germany and not return.

Chapter 2

The Build-up to War
April to August 1939

Paul departed from Vienna's Aspern Airfield on Tuesday, 25 April 1939 on the 3.30 pm KLM flight to Rotterdam, connecting to London. Paula and Hans were at the airport to see him off. It had been a heavenly day in Vienna as he left, but en route, the weather had worsened and turned into a snowstorm; the plane had to go up to an unusually high altitude, and everyone on board except Paul, a flight attendant and a baby became airsick.

Walter's fiancée, Lilly, stuck in London waiting for her US visa, which had been delayed, was at the airport to meet Paul and to give him the train fare into London. She was shocked that Paula was not with him. It was late by the time he arrived at his accommodation for the night, at the home of a sister of Mrs Humphris in London. Paula managed to call Paul that night, despite the late hour.

Initially, for a couple of days in London, Paul was upbeat, spending time with Lilly, trying to help with her visa issue, and visiting an uncle who had recently made it to London. On the weekend, he travelled north to Kidderminster to join Olga, and to begin work for Mr and

The Build-up to War

Mrs Humphris. For the first couple of weeks he sent encouraging reports. The family, including the children, were welcoming. He was required to work in the extensive garden, which was neglected and overgrown, to clean out the garage, to make cots for the children. 'I'm working like a dog here, only physical work, just to pretend at least to myself that I don't eat the bread of charity for free,' he wrote. The hard physical labour kept his mind off his growing concern for those left behind in Vienna. He had heard the worrying news from Paula of the new regulation revoking tenancy protection for Jews, which meant they could be evicted from their long-term apartments, the only housing then available to them being overcrowded Jewish communal housing. Moreover, Paul was conscious of the 'crushingly hopeless' situation of his mother and Paula's parents. No countries were accepting immigrants who were beyond working age. His despair was intense: 'At night I have to bite the pillow [to stop crying out],' he wrote.

Little of this, though, was communicated in his daily letters to Paula. He was shocked at Olga's condition. According to Paula, reflecting on this period two years later, 'Paul was shaken the first time that he saw her, to find her an old, worn out, broken woman'. She was forty. But at first he didn't disclose his reaction to Paula, even though her intuition immediately told her that something was wrong, and she imagined it must be to do with Olga:

> *Today the first letter arrived from him from Kidderminster. The letters from London were all rather cheerful, he told me everything that had happened, talked about the people with whom he was in contact and altogether seemed fine. Today's letter from Kidderminster didn't really say anything in particular. Either's Olga's looks or Olga's mental status or something else there must be so awful that he could only squeeze out*

a couple of words. He seems to be desperately worried. I'm burning for his next letter and hope to be able to read more about what's going on.

Paula couldn't share her anxiety with anyone other than her younger brother, far away in New York. Paul's letters to Paula in the following days seemed more reassuring, though still not mentioning anything about Olga's condition: he was enjoying the heavy work and the host family were kind; the only problem was they were far away from Lilly in London and Minka, another friend from Vienna, in Exeter. To Walter, in contrast, Paul was more honest:

Olga looks like a corpse on holiday … she's unfortunately a completely unworldly person who spends her energy on everyone without thinking whether the person she's doing it for is worth it or not. In Vienna there was Paula, sometimes me too, who could set her straight. Here she was let loose among people whom one could best call worthless charlatans. The people pretend to be friendly but work Olga to death. She literally didn't get 5 hours of sleep in 24 before I got here. I could go on. The situation is disgusting and there's nothing to be done.

As for the possibility of finding a safe destination, Paul maintained a stoical awareness of the arbitrariness of fate. Possibility after possibility was still being explored, but to no avail: Australia, the US, Manila, Argentina. 'There's nothing we can do about it,' he wrote to Walter. 'Wait, wait, wait, wait, one day it will come and the next it won't. Fate … I'm no closer than I was a year ago, only now I'm stuck here in England with my sister, and my wife and my mother in Vienna. Not one step further. But I'll only despair at the very end, even after I'm dead.'

'I really don't take anything so terribly tragically anymore,' he wrote a few days later. Or rather, the situation of exile and separation is 'tragic but unalterable. I have always resigned myself silently to the blows of my fate (and believe me, they were not few and not exactly gentle)'. He expressed his philosophical attitude poetically: 'After all, we are nothing more than a little ball of feathers that is pushed around, dented, shattered, straightened up, blown up, puffed up by someone or something to happiness or unhappiness.' The translation struggles to convey the poetry of the German. Paul was also realistic about the Vienna that had been left behind and likened it to something he had read:

> *I read a book about Russian emigrés, aristocrats, bourgeois etc. in Paris, who had had to leave Russia, for whom their new life was always an absolute unreality as long they always thought back to Russia – to a Russia that they had only ever constructed for themselves, because it wasn't the Russia they had actually known (otherwise they wouldn't have had to leave).*

He was unsentimental about England: 'I can take it or leave it.'

Throughout the spring and early summer of 1939, Paula, too, adopted a stoical attitude. There were days when she 'was plagued by a terrible fear of war'. She tried, nevertheless, not to be overwhelmed by her anxiety: 'You struggle to your feet again. You have to distract yourself artificially. You simply have to go on ... hopefully this awful situation will pass.' The visa issue was forefront in her mind: 'It is still unclear to me that we can go somewhere. For the moment I have no idea how to bring that about. But if God gives Paul a job ...'

In May, Paula was exploring contacts in Vienna with US connections to see if affidavits could be arranged for herself, Paul and Olga; she was occasionally able to speak to them both by phone. Her letters to her brother in New York were full of details of friends and acquaintances who had managed to get to the United States, in the hope that somehow they might be able to help. The parents, too, were keeping their hopes alive: 'Papa and Mama have already adjusted to your departure,' she wrote to Walter. 'I believe that they would prefer to set out for New York today, not tomorrow. They would even go to Australia. One slowly gets used to underestimating these distances!' Paul's mother, Paula's parents and Lilly's parents had started to learn English. Alice, Paula's older sister, was their teacher. She had been working as an English teacher, certainly with private students at home, and probably also for the Israelitische Kultusgemeinde (IKG), the Jewish community organisation, who had arranged English classes as part of their retraining programs for potential emigrants. She had thus become the breadwinner of the family, though the number of her students was falling off as people managed to depart.

The months dragged on without success. Australia as an option kept 'dangling' before Paul and Paula. In March, a guarantor had been found, which suggested that a permit was coming. Later that month it had still not arrived; by the middle of April the guarantor in Australia had written that a permit would be granted soon. But there were difficulties: Paula and Paul's mother had had refusals from Australia, meaning if Paul got a visa he would have to leave his mother behind, which he could not countenance. Moreover, Olga would not be allowed to practise medicine in Australia, and permanent separation from her was not something either Paul or Paula would contemplate. By May, Paul was beginning to feel that Australia was becoming impossible. He could see how badly Olga was coping on her own in London, another reason not to abandon her. And then there was a further, seemingly insurmountable obstacle – a landing fee of £200, the equivalent of $20,000 today, a prohibitive amount. Yet in August, Paula was still holding out hope, waiting for a response from Australia to Paul's application, perhaps prompted by the departure for Sydney of her close friend Martha Müller's mother that month (with Martha planning to follow immediately) – and Paula knew that following the Müllers, if that was at all possible, was Paul's preference, rather than going to the US.

In June, Paula was submitting applications to go to Manila, where her aunt's family had managed to get a visa, but she was also exploring connections in Argentina and Canada. Other relatives and friends were in Brazil, Shanghai and Tokyo; others were trying to get to India or Burma (Myanmar). By early August, Paul had still not managed to find work and their application for Manila had been rejected. Paula seemed to take this calmly, but cautiously: 'It is really not a shame about Manila. Perhaps. Who knows ...' Nevertheless, it was clear to Paula by now that she needed be ready to leave at short notice, which involved getting a passport, a task that required elaborate interactions with the Nazi authorities: she was 'completely occupied with her preparations', according to her father. In addition, she was broadening her skills by taking a leatherworking course – the Jewish community organisation had been tasked by the Nazis, as part of their policy of compelling Jewish emigration, with establishing courses intended to reskill individuals who were hoping to emigrate. The daily public pressures, insults and attacks continued, though the family wrote very little about them for fear of attention from the authorities (official censorship, with letters from Vienna to foreign destinations being opened and resealed, appears to have begun in early September 1939 when the war began), as well as not wanting to further distress Walter. Occasionally details were communicated: Alice's dentist, who had always been friendly, abruptly refused to treat her, for example. Unusually, Alice communicated this explicitly: 'My dentist – she was so conveniently in the neighbourhood – has abandoned me on account of the J.,' she wrote.

Finally, in August, Paul managed to get approval to work as a chemical engineer in Bradford in lanolin production. And Paula's passport was about to be issued. So, there was progress on both fronts. But then a new hurdle and a new delay: Paula could not travel immediately on an original visitor's visa, which Paul had used in April; she would have to wait until she received a new visa, either as a domestic servant or on the basis of Paul's work visa. But time was running out for Paul to arrange a visa renewal or a new visa for Paula. More and more friends were leaving, for Trieste, for Budapest. The war would start in three weeks. By 19 August, 'Paul has not yet received my visa renewal. We will see if and when I can go to England.'

Paula spoke with Paul and Olga by phone that evening. Martha Müller's mother was in Antwerp visiting her sons, and was due to leave from Genoa, en route for Australia, on 23 August. Martha was planning to leave for England shortly, though it would take another fortnight for all her papers to be in order. In the meantime, she had temporarily moved in with Paula and her parents, sleeping in the family living room, now that her own family home had been given up. 'Unfortunately, I will not get away so quickly. It would have been nice if we had been able to travel together,' Paula wrote. By 21 August, Paula's visa had still not arrived. She was under intense pressure as the threat of war loomed ever closer: 'I have become very small and scatterbrained,' she wrote. Yet she still managed to sound optimistic: 'But in a few weeks I will certainly be in England' – if only they had known.

Chapter 3

The Outbreak of War

September 1939 to May 1940

It was only in the final week before the outbreak of war on 1 September that a realistic appraisal of the situation became unavoidable. Earlier, in July, Hans had received affidavits for himself, his non-Jewish wife, Lisl, and Alice; their sponsors were wealthy and influential members of the New York Sephardic community. The affidavits were, of course, only part of the story, as there was a mountain of other paperwork to organise before a completed visa application could be submitted. This delay apparently suited both Hans, who was in no hurry to leave as he had a good job and as well had to manage the forced relocation from the home he had lived in for over a decade into a new apartment, and Alice, who was reluctant to abandon her English language students. 'Until later we still have time,' Hans wrote to his brother. Their parents remained optimistic: 'Everyone, with Papa leading, diligently studies English, makes arrangements and plans ahead, and absolutely wants to see you both again in America,' wrote Paula. Papa was similarly relaxed: 'There is no rush with our American journey. We are young and can wait,' he wrote good-humouredly. By 27 August, as the crisis over Poland grew, he adopted a more sober tone in a letter to his son in New York:

> *One cannot foresee anything in view of the threatening situation. We still always hope that a means will be found to keep the peace and to enable quiet to return again to Europe. God grant it. But, nevertheless, if what we fear comes about and with that our exchange of letters is interrupted, then it will remain for us to be brave and confident … We are all healthy and well and confident that God will also help and protect us. Things can still come good after all, and we remain hopeful to remain in contact. But if it happens otherwise, then you, like us, will look forward to the return of better times.*

The following day he expressed somewhat more hopeful sentiments: 'Hopefully in a couple of days everything will be quiet again and the black clouds will disperse.'

Walter and Lilly, whose visa had finally come through after months of delay in England and who had arrived in New York, were to be married in a few days, and the impending wedding inspired the need for the family in Vienna to sound upbeat to reassure them and not to destroy their happiness. The bland tone of the family letters to Walter – 'no news here' – belied an increasingly disastrous situation. On 7 September, less than a week after hostilities had begun, Paula's uncle and aunt died by suicide in their apartment; their bodies were found by Hans. Walter learnt about it only six months later: 'I did not tell you about it so as not to trouble the beautiful days of your wedding,' his mother wrote. Paula then explained the circumstances:

Concerning Uncle Julius and Paula [her aunt was also named Paula], *I will tell you a bit more. She had suffered for many years and always wanted to commit suicide. He was terribly worn down by their life together with her. When I saw him the last time shortly before his death, I was shaken all day by the look in his eyes. He had suffered unspeakably. One really expected from day to day that he would end it. He wrote a letter in which he explained everything and ordered and prepared everything in advance with his accustomed exactitude. He wrote that Hanni* [their daughter, who had made it to Shanghai] *is engaged and so does not need them anymore, and so he can finally go to his rest. They both poisoned themselves with gas in September. It is tragic that a letter to them from Hanni arrived a few days later saying that the engagement had been broken off. This poor girl is left all alone in the world.*

Although the exact circumstances of suicide are always personal, it was becoming more prevalent among Jews in Vienna, as the statistics showed.

On 28 August, Paula spoke to Paul and Olga in England for the last time. Paul's mother joined the call – her last chance to speak to her children. On 1 September Germany invaded Poland; England declared war on the 3rd, destroying any hope of Paula joining Paul there. They were separated. Regular letters from Paul continued to arrive until the 3rd, but already by the 6th Paula was suffering by not hearing from him, as there could be no direct mail service between England and Germany, now at war. Communication between them from this point depended on others: on 15 September, Paula heard that Paul and Olga had written to a relative of Paula's in Amsterdam, but frustratingly the relative did not forward their letter, just the simple message that they were well. Paul was able to write to Walter, however he did not forward the letters to Paula, which led her to suspect that Paul was not communicating the reality of his feelings to her: 'Are Paul's letters not such that you can send them to me to read?' she asked. The question of communication remained a persistent issue.

The outbreak of war changed Paul's status. Within a few days of arriving in England in late April 1939 to join Olga in Kidderminster, he had registered with the police as an 'alien', as he was required to do, and on 3 May was issued with an Aliens Registration Card at the office in Stourbridge, Worcestershire. The card contained a copy of his passport and passport photo, and a record of his address, which was updated when he moved to start work in Bradford in 1940: one of the obligations of foreign residents in the UK was to report every change of address to the local police within a few days and have that entered onto the individual's Registration Card. At the outbreak of war, his possession of a German passport meant that he was reclassified as an 'enemy alien', one of about 70,000 from Germany and Austria residing in Britain at that time. He was to be assessed by a local tribunal established for the classification of enemy aliens in terms of the threat they were thought to represent. Those classified as Category A, seen as constituting an imminent threat, were to be interned immediately, although this constituted only 1 per cent of those examined.

There was a risk that Paul might have been so classified, as one criterion was 'special knowledge of chemistry'. Those assessed as Category B – who were seen as a potential, but not immediate, threat – were not interned at first but were subject to restrictions. Refugees were mostly classified as Category C, meaning they would remain at liberty. This represented about 90 per cent of 'enemy aliens', most of them Jewish. In addition to these classifications, an assessment was made as to whether the person was a refugee from Nazi persecution. Perhaps because of this, Paul was classified as B, which meant that he could keep working, albeit with restrictions on his movements (no further than 5 miles without police permission). Paul was one of 3200 men classified as B, of whom two-thirds were also classified as 'refugees from Nazi oppression'. But even this classification was harsh, as of the 225 male chemists or those working in the chemical industry who were assessed, about three-quarters were classified C. It is not clear whether Paul was able to, or chose to, communicate this to Paula.

He continued to receive news about Paula via Martha's brothers in Antwerp and relatives in Amsterdam. About his own situation, 'I am not at all in need of consolation,' he wrote to Walter. 'I live in a free country, unimaginable that there is something like this after our life in Vienna.' Yet the failure to be reunited with Paula and to rescue his mother was seen as another imponderable blow of fate, to be borne like the rest: 'Please don't feel sorry for me, right?' Paul went on. 'Sad? I no longer know what sad is because I really no longer know what happiness is or rather, what's not sad. It's all somehow become unimaginably incomprehensible to me and you accept it and bear it as long as you can. For certain, one day this will all be over. So I'm not sad, at most you can call it "stupid".' (Paul used the English word to express his state of insensibility.)

He was ambivalent about Paula's decision to remain in Vienna: on the one hand, he conscientiously refrained from criticising her; on the other, he admitted to having a vested interest in her staying:

> *The fact that Paula is not with me is her own issue, she would have had plenty of opportunities to come here before the outbreak of the war,*

but it dragged on until it was no longer possible. If we come together again it's OK, if not it's also OK, everyone should be blessed in his own way and I'm not in favour of the husband exerting any pressure on his wife. Besides, there is something else that plays a role. My mother is still in Vienna and it gives me a certain amount of comfort to know that she is not dealing with the savages all by herself, but that Paula is sometimes with her too.

Paula's own reflections in her letters echoed this ambivalence. On the one hand, she wrote to Walter: 'It's turned out that you're the smartest and most foresighted. Hopefully we'll all come together once again.' On the other, she accepted the responsibility for the decision in April to stay temporarily with her parents and Paul's mother, which had now become permanent: 'You ask where Paula is? For the moment she is still here where she belongs.' Yet she recognised the implications of the decision: 'Hopefully I'll still be together with Paul and Olga again. And if not, I'll be having to say to myself that it's my own fault.' The fateful consequences of a wrong decision haunted her: 'You simply can't afford to make mistakes. Nothing will ever be quite right again once you've done the wrong thing.'

By 24 September, Paula had finally had a letter from Paul, reassuring her about himself and Olga. Things were not so reassuring in Vienna: a young friend had died by suicide that same day, with a large funeral at the Central Cemetery held a few days later. Letters from Paul via friends continued to arrive at irregular intervals. By October, news had begun to circulate of plans for deportation of Jews to Nisko in Poland, initially only younger, healthy males to begin building an infrastructure that would allow for resettlement of the rest in abandoned villages there. Publicly, at least, this was not initially considered threatening:

'The matter about Poland is judged relatively favourably by all the leaders,' Paula wrote. Privately, though, the frightening significance of this development was clear to her, although, aware of censorship of foreign mail, she avoided any hint of criticism: 'Here there are relocation projects which have been generously started. Retirees, etc., are not a priority for now. There are only two emigration goals: USA or Poland.' The longer-term implications for those staying in Vienna were, however, clear: 'What this means for me is questionable … we and all our relatives may move in a few months …' Hans' situation, though, was different. His wife, Lisl, was not Jewish, and he was now working for the Jewish community organisation (before the Anschluss he had been a businessman), both factors protecting him for the time being: 'The matter about which I wrote to you in the last letter doesn't affect Hans. Not for anyone who lives in such a marriage. And because of his current position.' As for herself, 'I got a letter from Paul written ten days ago, externally things seem to be going well for him. Internally, probably like me,' she wrote.

Indeed, Paul was deeply aware of the implications of the beginning of deportations. He wrote to Walter in early November from Bradford:

> *If your wife still wants her parents to come to you, she must hurry, because there's a campaign already underway for the removal of all the German Jews to Poland. The Jewish community organisation has been put in charge and its people are already going with transports to the East. Young people are being taken there first, the older ones following. Old people and pensioners still have a few months ahead of them. Given the thoroughness and rapidity with which this is being carried out, I believe that Paula's turn will soon come up, too. So, I ask you, since I can do nothing from here, to leave no stone unturned*

> *in obtaining affidavits. As for my mother, unfortunately, I don't know of any possible escape.*

He reinforced the point in a letter only a couple of days later:

> *This is not simply forced labour, it's a preliminary resettlement operation for all the Jews. Of course, we don't know what will happen to emigration from there (if such an emigration is ever possible again). Your whole family, including Paula, is of course also affected by this and Hans is naturally making every effort to obtain affidavits. But he's unlikely to succeed before the catastrophe. Unfortunately, it wasn't possible for me to get Paula and my mother here before the outbreak of war, because I obtained my work permit only shortly before that. What will happen with my mother is of course nightmarish.*

Paula echoed his words, with resignation: 'I hear from Paul that he has now got work, in fact in his specialty area, which is wonderful. But if it had only happened a little earlier, both of us (his mother and I) would now be with them. But it wasn't to be.' Paul's move to Bradford made her particularly anxious about Olga, with whom she reproached Walter for not staying in contact: 'I don't know why you haven't written a single time to Ollie. Even in letters to me she only writes a short greeting. I believe she's so exhausted that she can scarcely go on. And now Paul isn't with her anymore. She's been afflicted in body and soul since August '38. And even before that she'd had a bad time. If only I could be with them.' A few weeks later little had changed: 'She is very weakened and completely crushed by unhappiness.'

With the threat of deportation ever closer, Paula found herself preoccupied with endlessly pursuing whatever diminishing chances there were of being able to leave, errands to 'take care of all sorts of family matters', and maintaining networks of friends and contacts. Her more difficult tasks included comforting a friend's mother, whose husband had just died by suicide. This selfless work for her parents and Paul's mother, and other friends, had its own reward, but it was no longer enough: 'On the whole and in general, it's often been good that I've been here. There's always been something to take care of, to arrange. It's sometimes also been a happiness. Now, though, it's soon enough. Now I'd like very much to go to Paul. But I still have to wait.' Both her brothers, Walter in New York, Hans still in Vienna, focused on trying to get her a visa for somewhere, anywhere, especially for the US, monumentally difficult as that was. There were various tantalising but potentially futile possibilities within Europe:

> *Paul's cousin joined his father in Belgium three weeks ago and is making efforts to bring me there. I still don't know whether it makes a lot of sense for me to sit alone in Belgium. I think it's impossible to go any further from there. What do you think of this plan? I must say that I really don't know what I should do. Assuming the Polish thing doesn't happen, I wouldn't in any case go to Belgium alone.*

A week later she had abandoned the idea. There were similar considerations about Italy, which at this time had not yet joined the war: relatives and friends had gone there in the hope that they could go further, but in the end had to return to Vienna when their visas expired. Another fruitless lead. In December, however, Walter had managed to get affidavits for the US for his parents-in-law, which occasioned great joy. Yet one affidavit was then lost in the mail to Vienna, causing further delays.

As the bitterly cold winter of 1939–40 set in and food shortages became apparent, there was another blow. In early January, Paula's older sister, Alice, became ill with a severe flu and died within a few days; she had a weak heart. She was forty-eight. The family was devastated with grief. And to make matters worse, their sole source of income, Alice's English teaching, was now gone. As 1940 began, the Nazi authorities put the deportations to Poland on hold until they could be better organised and continued to pressure Jews to leave. These first few months of the year were a kind of unsettling hiatus, full of stress and grief over Alice's death; both Paula and her mother were losing weight. Mail from America was very slow, delayed by the severe weather and further slowed down by the censorship process. Paul's mother had been forced out of the family home in Novaragasse and had come to live with them, occupying Alice's old room: 'Paula won't have to go running to see her at her old place anymore,' her father wrote. Martha Müller was now living permanently with Paula and her family, having narrowly failed to get away to England in time before the outbreak of war. And Hans looked as if he might get a visa for Manila with the help of relatives, and was planning to go if it came through, though he still preferred to remain in Vienna. Paula wrote to Walter:

> *I'm sitting now in your little room, at your little round table, the sun is shining, only you're not here. You can imagine how much we miss you. I have almost no social visiting rounds any more. Most people have left already, and when you're burdened and oppressed, you can only bear very few people … Our parents are terribly quiet. If, for example, you leave Papa alone for an hour he rummages through his books and has red and swollen eyes. But he's left alone only a little. Now Hans is leaving in the next few months. That sadly will be a*

new blow. Alice wouldn't have travelled away from our parents under any circumstance. Papa doesn't want to leave any more. He wants to remain near Alice. Although he's specially attached to you, always speaks of you both with longing, waits for your letters – he remains with Alice.

The presence of Paul's mother, Mathilde, was a comfort: 'We are very glad that Paul's mother is with us. She takes care of herself and does embroidery the whole day, and it's a diversion from our thoughts, especially for Papa who otherwise would sit all alone in the room the whole morning,' wrote Paula's mother, Tonie. Paula's father adopted a more resigned tone in his letter: 'The inconceivable ability of people to become accustomed to such sad, unchangeable conditions helps us a bit to put this sadness behind us. One sleeps, one eats and drinks, and one goes firmly onwards, only one cannot be cheerful anymore, we are already too old for that. But whatever God wills!' As for Paula, 'I don't need to say how much I would like to be with you', she wrote. 'But if Hans also leaves, what would happen with the three old people, who would be utterly alone? I tell you, I already have entirely white hair, but with all the brooding, nothing shows on the outside.'

Paul, too, was finding the separation terribly hard. He visited Olga at Christmas and Easter (a four-hour journey from Bradford on the express train), finding her in a terrible state:

She's become a wreck, unrecognisably exhausted, tired, tired, tired. I wasn't in a position before this to make her see reason and let go of this immense amount of work and responsibility that she's taken on, to look for easier work without suffocating responsibility or to move here and live modestly with me. Now the situation's come to a head

> *in the last few days, there was a heated argument with her boss, she simply can't continue, so she'll come to me soon, and we'll somehow manage to live one day at a time.*

The only solution that Paul could see was for Olga to be reunited in the US with Paula, 'who is not only very, very wise, but who also has a good real-life influence on my sister'. So, Paul made a tentative request: 'I'm no grave-robber,' he said, but the fact was that Alice's death meant that the affidavit Walter had managed to secure for her was not needed: could it somehow be transferred to Olga? 'The dance lurches on,' he wrote. 'I've told you only the naked facts, I'm no longer in a condition to untangle them.'

Walter didn't need to do this, as at about the same time as Alice's death, he wrote that there was a chance of obtaining affidavits each for Paul and Paula. The news of which was received with mixed feelings on both their parts. For Paula, it would allow an application in her own right, but she doubted how useful it would be for her, given that her place of birth (Bucharest) meant that she was subject to the small Romanian quota for the United States: 'My chances and prospects are very poor. The Romanian quota will only [be]come current in a couple of years. Perhaps you have a good idea how I could come to you?' she wrote.

Paul had similar ambivalence, torn between his need not to abandon Olga, his need to get Paula out of Vienna and his initial reluctance to go to the United States if there were any alternative. There was also the question of his employment. He summarised the complexities to Walter, referring to Paula by her nickname 'Bulli':

> *I only pray that Bulli will be able to start something with her affidavit. Maybe she can go to Holland with it and from there can come here,*

or otherwise somewhere. As grateful as I am to you for this affidavit (and I mean that sincerely), coming to you is out of the question for me for the time being. There is an absolute barrier: I will not leave my sister this time even if (this is not a hollow statement) we both perish as a result. As I've said, we'll try every possible thing to get Bulli, if not here, then at least to you.

Imagining Walter's reaction to Paul's acknowledgement of his likely ongoing separation from Paula, he went on to reassure him:

Please, don't take what I've said about my not going with Bulli as somehow frivolous. Only I know how much I love her and how much I suffer under this separation (I've always been a decent guy and I'll always be one, but fate just hasn't seen it that way). I can't leave my sister alone.

He learnt via Martha Müller's brother in Antwerp that Paula was still exploring possibilities of joining an uncle who had left Vienna for Milan; she had managed to secure a six-month visa for that purpose. Paul considered this move unwise, that the situation was more dangerous than it had been only two months earlier: 'My wife is doing everything possible to try to get to Alfred in Milan and then to get here from there. First of all, I think it's impracticable, and who can say what the political situation will be tomorrow. I think that's as far as private travel can go.' He added in a subsequent letter that 'going to Alfred is greater madness these days than it might have been two months ago. I'll just wait, wait, wait, even if it's only at the Last Judgement that we meet again'. He saw this period as 'the calm at the centre of the whirlwind'. It was indeed, as circumstances soon proved.

Meanwhile, in Vienna, the family's grief over the death of Alice was unabated. Paula's task was to commission a headstone from a stonemason for the grave:

> *I have chosen a beautiful headstone for our Alice. It's rose-veined marble. And very beautiful in shape. Instead of a mound, there will be a plate on the grave so that it doesn't look so uncared for, like so many other graves, which must be left behind. And behind the stone there'll be a climbing rose. It'll all be finished in a few weeks, and then I'll send you a photo. I was at her grave this year on my birthday. She was always with me on that day – but this time I had to go to her.*

Paula's daily routine of visits to support friends continued, particularly to elderly people who had been left behind and were getting used to loneliness. Lilly's grandmother, Regine, known in the family as Omama, had recently been removed to the main Jewish old people's home in Seegasse in the 9th district, in preparation for her daughter's eventual departure for America; Paula visited her there regularly. She saw Hans often, too, at work in the Jewish Community Organisation building, the former synagogue where she and Paul had been married.

Chapter 4

Internment and Deportation

May to July 1940

Suddenly, in England, in May 1940 everything changed, as Britain and all its Allies experienced a series of disastrous military defeats. The 'phoney war' had come to an end in early April 1940 when Britain failed to prevent German occupation of Norway. The reporting of the fighting in Norway was accompanied by a campaign in the press about the threat of a 'fifth column', an expression that had emerged in the context of the Spanish Civil War. Local supporters of the Nazis on the ground in Norway had undermined the capacity of the country to defend itself, it was argued. There ensued the German invasion of the Netherlands, Belgium and France, which began on 10 May. The resulting threat to Britain became clear to the Cabinet, now led by Churchill, who had become prime minister that same day. The situation became more and more grave as the German forces quickly advanced; the British forces in Belgium were surrounded, and evacuations from Dunkirk began; by 22 June, France had signed a surrender. Britain was now fighting for its life, essentially alone

(Belgium, the Netherlands and Denmark all having surrendered), and was unable to count on American support; an invasion appeared imminent.

In this critical situation, those who were distrustful of all German passport holders, regardless of their reasons for being in Britain, came to prevail. Paul was caught up in the sudden panic. A wider internment was authorised: on 12 May, a round-up was ordered of males with a German passport (regardless of their classification) residing near the coast, particularly in the south and southeast, where the risk of subversion in the event of an invasion was greatest. For the first time, large numbers of those recognised as refugees were to be interned. On 15 May, the Home Office ordered the internment of all those in Category B. Paul was arrested the following day. He was taken temporarily to Uniacke Barracks in Harrogate, not far from Bradford. Olga, who by now was living with Paul in Bradford, wrote immediately to New York, telling Walter and Lilly of this development, but asking them not to let the family in Vienna know yet. 'He has been interned yesterday in the morning,' she wrote (now routinely in English).

> *The papers and the wireless say it's only temporary and his boss hopes to get him out, because he needs him very badly. I am absolutely certain that he will be all right and it is thousand times better to be interned in England than to live in "freedom" in Germany – but it is hard anyhow. I am hopeful and in the long run they will realise how Paul stands to this country which has given him shelter and bread after his terrible time in Vienna.*

Paul's arrest had severe implications for Olga.

You can imagine how I feel alone in this city. I know only two little girls, my health isn't good at all and to know how Paul will feel about me. My dream is still to do any useful work but I haven't got any chance yet. I am not able to do hard work and so I do not know what will happen to me when Paul doesn't come soon.

Communication continued to be a major problem in this difficult and urgent situation, intensifying the distress. Paul had increasingly limited ability to communicate his whereabouts, and communication between England and Vienna had to go via the US, now that postal services via contacts in the Netherlands, Belgium and even France were no longer available. Paula had no idea of what was happening: Olga had asked Walter not to say anything to her yet about Paul's internment, and in any case the mail via the US could be very slow and intermittent. Three weeks after Paul's internment Olga remained optimistic:

Paul is quite all right, only worried about me ... He is all right, I am certain about this, perhaps he will get free from the internment. I hope so in any case, he did useful work and his boss does all he can for him, and if not, we will keep calm and in good spirits. I intend to go to my aunt in Cardiff for a few weeks and then look for a job. I wait only another week or so how Paul's things stand.

Grete, the aunt with whom Paul and Paula had shared the apartment in the Litoralishof, had managed to escape to Britain and was living in Cardiff. By the following day, Olga was less sanguine: she had not heard from Paul now for a week, and only knew that he was no longer where he had been detained. 'I believe that we all will be interned,' she wrote, 'it doesn't matter to me, only that all contact with you probably will end ... But head high and courage! The Nazis will lose the war and then the world will be released from their terror! Whether we will survive is no matter.' (By now, Category B women with German passports were indeed being interned as well as men, so Olga's concern was realistic; she herself was Category C.) A fortnight later, she reported simply that 'Paul is all right', and that she had finally managed to find some more domestic employment, although she continued to regret the waste of her talents as a paediatrician.

On 5 June, three weeks after his internment, Paul had written to Walter, now in English, as the letters were censored, and letters in German would invite more scrutiny, and perhaps take longer to be delivered. In the letter, Paul disguised the location of people who were now in an 'enemy country', in this case Vienna, by references to Walter meeting them (rather than hearing from them). Paula's gender was also changed (to Paul) to obscure his relationship with someone in an enemy country. Paul felt utterly helpless in his concern for Olga and Paula, made worse by the impossibility of communicating with them.

Dear Bobby,

It's about one month that I want to write to you. Since 3 weeks I am in this camp and as I thought I will be soon back in Bradford I did not wrote. Now I see that I have to change my mind. When you will answer this letter please put under the above written address the words "please forward" because it is nearly for certain that we shall be moved from here. As far as I remember I wrote in my last letter that Olga came to me so about 2 months ago in a very bad state of health. I had to leave her and from this time I have no idea of her whereabout. There is not much to report. I am very well, plenty and good food. Only my brain is already a little bit broken. Yes dear Bobby it is sometimes difficult to keep smiling but we have to carry on till to the last. Beside this problem what will happen with Olga, I have no letter from Paul. On the 26th May was Paul's birthday, again without me, I think so a fortnight ago there was Gretes wedding. And the world goes on. Do you sometimes meet Mathilde or Tonie or Martin? Please write me as soon as possible, only a few words on a post-card. Remember me to Lilly.

Your Paul

Shortly afterwards, he was transferred to an internment site that was intended to be more permanent, the recently opened Onchan Internment Camp near Douglas on the Isle of Man. Holiday accommodation on the Isle of Man had been requisitioned, a policy that was reluctantly accepted by the local inhabitants, given that its tourism business had been devastated by the outbreak of war, and they would be paid for the use of their accommodation. Onchan consisted of a series of Edwardian and Victorian boarding houses facing the sea, hastily surrounded by barbed wire. Reports and memoirs suggest that conditions in the camp were somewhat uncomfortable but not oppressive; Onchan was overcrowded, with two men to a bed. One internee, Kurt Fischer, remembered:

> The camp was surrounded by beautiful scenery. In the distance, on one side, a castle could be seen while on another side, where the barbed-wire fence bordered a cobble-stoned street, pedestrians from a nearby village used to stop to have short conversations

with us. On Sundays the whole village would assemble at the fence; whilst some conversed with us, most of them regarded us as if we were foreign animals in a zoo.

The internees were generally treated with respect and allowed considerable latitude in organising activities for themselves, including giving lectures, given the large number of highly trained and skilled individuals among them. There was considerable anxiety about a possible German attack on Britain from Ireland, officially neutral but no friend to Britain, in which case the Isle of Man with its 2000 mainly Jewish internees would be captured. There were suicidal thoughts. Communication with the outside world was restricted, and no radios or newspapers were allowed. Paul was initially unable to communicate to Olga, and hence to Walter and Paula, his whereabouts or his situation, or what was about to transpire.

On 10 July Olga received a telegram from Paul: 'Leaving today, destination Canada.' She wrote to Walter: 'Paul has gone to Canada … As soon as I hear from him I will let you know.' But the weeks went by without Olga hearing any further. A month later: 'Nothing from Paul. If you hear by any chance from him, please wire to me. It is almost more than I can bear.' After another fortnight: 'I am well, my greatest sorrow is Paul, I haven't heard from him since he left this country. May God help us.' And a month later: 'I wrote you twice or three times that Paul went to Canada, perhaps you can get an information through the Red Cross.' Walter contacted officials in Canada to try to determine if Paul had been transferred there, even sending a prepaid return postal coupon, and waited for a reply.

Paula had remained unaware of Paul's internment for weeks, months. In July, a week after his departure from the Isle of Man, she wrote asking if Walter had heard anything from him and Olga, as she had heard they were no longer living together – but clearly had no idea of the reason why. 'For weeks we have been without news from you. This is very sad for us. Hopefully you and Pauli and Olli are healthy. We haven't heard from them for a very long time.' The lack of news continued to haunt her, and she wondered by early August if Walter was keeping something from her:

> *It's two years since Ollie left, on the 28th it'll be a year since I last spoke with Pauli and Olli by telephone. When will I hear their voices again? What is the news about Olli and Pauli's meeting? I miss, Walter, your normal detailedness. You can imagine that every word is important to me. And there's no point in silence or glossing over things, either.*

Yet Walter continued to try to honour Olga's wish to protect Paula from knowing about Paul's situation. He claimed not to have Olga's current address and not to have heard from her for a year and a half, but Paula found this inconsistent with what he had previously said and encouraged him to persist in trying to get in touch with Olga.

Finally, in late August, three months after Paul's internment, Paula received her first letter from Walter in several months, in which he disclosed some of the facts: that Paul had been interned and might be leaving for Canada. Paula reproached him for holding back this information: 'You want to comfort and soothe me. But a report of the facts while they are still fresh is best.' Many things were still unclear – was Olga in touch with Paul? Was she still living in Bradford, in Paul's old place? Would he have enough clothing for the winter? Was he properly fed? She was under the impression that Paul was still in England, and that perhaps Olga could send him food. Gustav

Brössler, a friend who had been in touch with Paul and Olga in England, was arriving in the US soon – perhaps he would have reports. 'Please stay in touch with Olli. I fear so much for them both,' she concluded.

Near the end of September, on Paul's birthday, she still had heard nothing from either of them: 'This morning I went out with Mathilde. Today is Paul's birthday. A particularly difficult day for her, so I wanted her to think about other things. She's in fact extraordinarily brave. She's worried sick about Olga, who is so utterly alone. I can't understand how Olga hasn't heard anything from her brother either.' 'My hair has already gone almost completely white,' she added. She was forty-three. 'We're all healthy and that's the main thing, right? If only I knew that about them both'. But the news from their friend Brössler, recently arrived in the US from England, when it came, was far from the simple report on the whereabouts and wellbeing of Paul and Olga that Paula had hoped for. In a letter to Walter on 11 October, Hans wrote:

> *A letter just arrived from Mr. Gustav Brössler in which he writes: "Paul may, so we fear, not be alive any longer." Write to me immediately and in detail if and what you know. If you know something about his departure, or if (and what) Olga has written about it. Or if news from Mr. Brössler is based only on assumptions and does not have any positive basis. I'd especially like to know if Mr. Brössler knows anything positive about Paul's journey or about a portion of the trip, if so, how far they were together. It is also important to know if Paul's is an ocean journey and whether anyone knows on which ship. For the moment we've said nothing to Paula. Answer immediately.*

Brössler's fear was not without basis: on 2 July, the ship the *Arandora Star*, carrying internees to Canada, had been sunk by an enemy torpedo in the Atlantic off the coast of Scotland, with the loss of 805 lives, almost half the people on board. Was Paul among them?

Chapter 5

Dunera

July to September 1940

Amid the crisis of May 1940, a new, far more serious fate than internment loomed. As early as 24 May, Churchill had expressed his desire that internees, especially those classified as Category A, be deported, as they were thought, rightly or wrongly, to be a security risk in the event of an invasion; there were many arbitrary and unfair decisions about degree of risk. The idea of deporting internees was a highly controversial measure, strenuously opposed by the United States, on the grounds of likely retaliation by Germany against internees from Allied countries once they got to Germany (although at this stage the United States was not at war, it was the guarantor of the welfare of British prisoners of war and other internees in Germany).

There was a second, practical grounds for supporting deportation: it became increasingly clear that, as the net of internment widened, the number of internees was seriously outgrowing the capacity of the authorities to accommodate them. For example, on 16 May, all male Category B enemy aliens, roughly 3000, had been interned; by the 27th, this had been extended to female Category B enemy aliens, some

3600, half of whom had left Germany because of the impact of the anti-Jewish Nuremberg Laws. On 31 May, the internment of Category C was permitted, at the discretion of the security services and the police. Italy joined the war on 10 June, which meant that 19,000 Italians in Britain were now classified as enemy aliens. By early June, requests had already been made to the Canadian and Australian governments to take several thousand high-risk internees. The British proposal was accepted only with caution and on a provisional basis by the Canadian Government, which was reassured that those chosen for deportation would be regarded by the British authorities as the most dangerous; that is, those classified as A, as well as prisoners of war.

The argument for deportation on the grounds of national security, and because by now all enemy aliens had become suspect, obscured the fact that there was a need to deport simply to reduce numbers; the German blockade of Britain meant that food supplies were an issue, too. The result was that the decision as to who exactly would be deported became more and more indiscriminate; it was left in the hands of the military authorities guarding the internees, who had little idea of who was who (the Home Office, not the War Office, was in charge of classification). Many of the internees for deportation were thus chosen randomly.

The first deportations, to Canada, commenced on 20 June 1940. The second of these ships to sail was the ill-fated *Arandora Star*. Its sinking underlined how problematic the policy of deportations was (German retaliations were again feared), made more so when it gradually emerged that the ship's cohort of deportees included refugees. The ensuing scandal led to a cessation of deportations to Canada, although not immediately, as two further shiploads left in the days immediately following the sinking, before the policy changed.

Fate was not on Paul's side. He was among the first to be caught up in the new developments: chosen as one of 2000 refugees to be included in the next sailing, presumably for Canada, as no ships had yet sailed for Australia. To increase the number of volunteers for deportation, various incentives were used: some men were promised release on arrival, and Canada was a destination Paul had contemplated as preferable to the US; its proximity to Walter in the US was also a possible factor. It is unlikely, however, that Paul volunteered given his concern about being separated from Olga and his preference for Australia. Only a small number of men, mostly married, with their wives in Britain, volunteered.

He was taken with other internees from the Isle of Man to the port of Liverpool and boarded the *Dunera* – but for where? They were not told where they were going, or they were given misleading information. The internees on board realised their likely destination only several days into the journey, when the position of stars, and the weather, meant that the route they were taking was incompatible with a trip to Canada: they were going to Australia.

Australia had initially agreed to accept internees, so when the Canadian avenue closed, Australia became the only possible destination. However, only a single ship went to Australia before the British Government stopped deportations entirely. On 27 July, Cabinet decided to halt the policy of internment, and a program of a slow release of internees in Britain was immediately implemented. A third of those interned had been released by the end of the year. But Paul was not in Britain to benefit from this official change of heart: he was on his way to internment in Australia.

*

Much has been written about the voyage of the *Dunera*. From the outset, the officers and soldiers responsible for guarding the internees behaved callously; even as they boarded the ship, the internees' possessions, few as they were, were systematically removed, and torn up or tossed away, including precious and irreplaceable address books and papers, such as the affidavits they had spent so much effort in obtaining. Valuables, including wedding rings and watches, were stolen. Conditions on board were oppressive, with overcrowding, internees being kept below deck in squalor, and allowed only brief opportunities for air and exercise. The *Dunera* almost met the same fate as that of the *Arandora Star*, narrowly escaping an attempted torpedo attack. They passed the wreckage from another ship that had not been so lucky.

Paul spoke little of his experience, despite its hardships, and without resentment. He saw the albatrosses that accompanied the ship on its voyage. Occasional remarks he made reflected what has been written about the *Dunera* voyage: he was forced to run across broken glass on deck; he noted the irony of the fact that the machine guns were directed inwards, towards the internees, rather than outwards; all his documents were taken, so that he was without addresses and contact details. 'On my voyage I lost my notebook,' he wrote shortly after his arrival in Sydney. But he maintained his resolutely clear-sighted attitude. 'Someone had got seasick, and had thrown up on the deck. One of the Tommies told me, "You, fucking Jew, clean it up". And for me that represented freedom,' he said many years later. His attitude reflected Olga's assessment: 'It is thousand times better to be interned in England than to live in "freedom" in Germany – but it is hard anyhow.'

The *Dunera* reached the port of Fremantle on the west coast of Australia on 27 August 1940, after nearly seven weeks at sea. Paul's arrival in Australia was officially recorded on that date. The *Dunera* then stopped briefly in Melbourne, where the Italian and Category A German internees disembarked, to be taken to a POW camp near Tatura, a small town in the north of Victoria, about 150 kilometres north of Melbourne. A further 100 internees, chosen at random, were also added to this group, probably because authorities knew there was not quite room for everyone in the camp they were heading to in New South Wales. The *Dunera* arrived in Sydney on 6 September. An overnight train took the internees to a camp in Hay in a remote part of New South Wales, 730 kilometres west of Sydney. There, Paul was formally interned in Australia:

> Order for Detention of Enemy Alien.
>
> AND WHEREAS I am of opinion that it is expedient in the interests of the public safety, the defence of the Commonwealth, or the efficient prosecution of the war that Paul KURZ, being an enemy alien on board His Majesty's Transport "Dunera", who has been sent from the United Kingdom to Australia for internment should be detained.
>
> NOW THEREFORE I do hereby order that the said Paul KURZ shall be detained.

Paul was consigned to Hut 11, Camp 8, where he was to spend the next nine months.

Chapter 6

Vienna

July to November 1940

In Vienna, Paula had no knowledge of Paul's situation. For months after his departure on the *Dunera*, she was only aware that he had been interned and might be sent to Canada. She was desperate for news, for which she was almost entirely reliant on Walter, but he was being discreet, at Olga's request, and writing seldom. She reproached him for his silence, and sensed he was keeping things from her: 'I am convinced that Olga has sent a little news when she can.' Paula was getting mail from exiled relatives and friends in Manila, in Tokyo, contacts that Walter claimed not to have heard from, even though she knew they had written to him. Another conduit was a contact in Bucharest (Romania only entered the war in November 1940, so there were mail services with the US and Vienna until then), but that contact had heard nothing from Walter, nor from Paul and Olga. Hans also reproached Walter for his silence:

Paula is cross that your reports about Paul and Olga are so short and laconic. Why haven't you written some details in your letters, whether they're together, where their letters are from, what they've written, or whether they're well? This is all news which you're allowed to write. So be somewhat more forthcoming and remember that Paula is anxious, and hungry for every bit of news.

Paula's sense of isolation, and the impossibility of her situation, was growing. 'Today's Sunday and that's always a bad day for me,' she wrote. 'It's terrible if you don't have anyone you belong to. At least I've still got a hope that at some point things will go better. But poor Ollie has no hope now. God help us.' In September, around the time Paul was arriving in Sydney, she wrote: 'Next week is Paul's birthday! What can I do? I'd already wanted to be with him for his birthday *last* year. It's good that I'm still with the parents, especially now, when Hans and Lisl will be leaving soon. But I sometimes think I'm going mad.' Indeed, it seemed likely that Hans and Lisl, despite failing to get a visa earlier, would be able to go to Manila, where his mother's youngest sister, Helene, and her family had found refuge. Their absence would mean another painful loss for the family.

Hans's preference for Manila over the United States meant that Paula's lingering hope that they would all one day be reunited in America was unlikely – 'What was always the most important to us both, remaining together as a family, means less for the two of them,' she told Walter, but as usual she was realistic. 'I think it would be better for Hans to begin in Manila than with you in New York … you know them both and know how difficult it is for them to adapt to the smallest change of circumstances. They'll both certainly find work in Manila and it may be the case that he'll quickly get into a better position there.' But fate was not in their hands: 'Above all, world events will have the last word for us all.' In fact, Hans remained ambivalent about leaving, telling Walter that Helene had not been encouraging about his chances of getting to Manila; he doubted he would ever receive an entry visa for the Philippines. As for the US, even though he had submitted all his paperwork months earlier and had not so far been rejected, and his quota number looked as if it might be coming up, there were a number of hurdles, such as not having a passport and needing financial support for the fares; quite apart from the fact that neither he nor his wife really wanted to go there. Even when visas for the Philippines were granted in October 1940, Hans took no action.

Meanwhile, Paula continued seeing family and friends; in September, there was even a visit from an aunt from Berlin. Her ill son had been transferred to Vienna and she was keen to move there to be near him, if she could find somewhere to live, which was increasingly difficult. During the same period, Paula continued with dressmaking and tailoring courses at the IKG and English lessons with Hansi, a close friend of Alice's. But she was increasingly turning inward for strength: 'I have learnt to pray,' she said. The slender hope of Paul being accepted to the US remained alive, just. Paul's documents had been submitted to the US Consulate-General in London. Paula commented on Walter's efforts in this regard: 'For myself it is all meaningless. But perhaps it may help Paul further.' Shortly after Paul's internment, however, Olga wrote to Walter that a letter from the consulate had come for Paul saying that the affidavit of support was insufficient because it was 'not substantiated by conclusive documentary evidence (in duplicate) of the sponsor's <u>present</u> financial position'. Paula, when she finally heard about this from Walter, reacted in despair: 'The situation with the affidavit is terribly sad. Paul has practically no chance now. The affidavit … was my single hope for him. He is a poor devil. God knows what sort of a state he is in. Unfortunately, he was never all that strong.'

Amid all this uncertainty and apprehension, another departure seemed imminent. Since Walter's engagement, Paula and her family had become close to Lilly's parents, Major and Mrs Neuhaus. At last, it seemed that the elaborate visa approval process, which would allow them to join their daughter and her husband, was entering the final stages. By September, they had had their medical examinations at the US consulate and were now anxiously awaiting news of the final decision. 'Unfortunately, now most people receive rejections,' Paula wrote. 'But they have a parents' affidavit, so perhaps they will be accepted.' But the decision from the US Consulate, when it came in late September 1940, was negative; if they wanted to get to America to join their daughter, they would have to start the process all over again.

Still no one knew where Paul was. Olga was beside herself: 'My greatest sorrow is Paul, I haven't heard from him since he left this country. God help us,' she wrote in August. The confusion of where he might be was particularly frustrating for Paula. After reviewing various contradictory details in Walter's letters, she concluded, 'I believe from all the evidence till now that none of you know anything at all about him, whether he is in Europe or in America, and that you only work on conjecture.' By mid-October, her worries had not been relieved: 'I wait eagerly for news from you, whether you know anything about Paul yet. A friend here certainly thinks that we can see from your letters that he is already in Canada. Unfortunately, I don't share this view.' A letter from Walter finally did arrive a few days later:

> *Now to your letter to me. This unfortunately shook me in several ways. You've shifted the fixed date by which you should have news from Paul from the middle of October (your last letter) to the end of November and then say that Olga should have news at this time. I'd very much*

like to know how you've calculated that, since you don't in fact know where he is ... These cares are insanely heavy to bear. I can vividly imagine Olga's state.

News of Paul's whereabouts finally reached Olga via a cable from Sydney on 24 September 1940, two and a half months after the misleading cable from early July indicating he was headed to Canada. She immediately wrote to Walter, informing him that Paul was in Sydney, and followed up with two further letters (she wrote to Walter weekly), without any response; mail was very slow, letters and cards from America were taking, at best, between three and four weeks to arrive; some letters and cards had arrived a year or more late. The news of Paul's actual whereabouts had thus not reached Vienna by 11 October, when Hans wrote to Walter with his disturbing report from Gustav Brössler about the possibility that Paul was no longer alive. When the letter from Hans reached Walter in November, he telegrammed an immediate reply: 'Paul completely healthy with Martha Müller's family.' The Müllers were in Sydney, and Paul by now was in remote western New South Wales, so this was somewhat misleading. Perhaps it was simply a misunderstanding on Walter's part, especially if the Müllers had helped send the cable; more likely it was an indirect way (because of censorship) of saying Paul was in Australia. It was some time before any further news from Paul himself was received.

Chapter 7

Hay

September 1940 to May 1941

Camp 8 at Hay, one of two more or less identical camps about a kilometre apart, had been purpose-built on a former rubbish dump to house the internees from the *Dunera*. The land around the small rural town of Hay on the Murrumbidgee River was relatively flat and featureless, and inhospitable, susceptible to prolonged hot dry weather and strong winds causing dust storms, occasionally punctuated by flooding rains. The camp consisted of thirty-six huts arranged either side of a central avenue, which contained a communal toilet, and ablution and laundry facilities. The site was surrounded by barbed wire. And there were watchtowers. Each hut housed a minimum of twenty-four men in bunks; most huts housed more. The internees were allowed to choose the hut where they would live.

Paul was in Hut 11. 'I found very nice comrades here,' he wrote to Walter. Bob Vogel, a fellow internee, wrote later: 'Everybody was free to choose whichever hut they wanted to go to. I was fortunate to get into a hut with a bunch of academics, some very nice people, one of whom turned out to be Paul Kurz. I was the youngest in camp.' (He was sixteen, and not actually the youngest). Another hut resident, Peter Tikotin, remembered that when Paul installed himself in the hut with the youngsters (Peter was nineteen) they were not happy to have an 'old guy' among them (Paul was just thirty-nine). 'He said he wouldn't get in their way, he would just do things to be helpful, and he began by picking up a broom and sweeping the layer of dust out of the hut.' 'Paul befriended me,' wrote Vogel many years later, 'and more or less became my second father. We walked around the barbed wire every night, and talked and discussed things and he was an enormous moral support.'

Communication with the outside world was slow and frustrating. On the same day that Paul arranged for a cable to be sent to Olga informing her of his whereabouts, 24 September 1940, he wrote to Walter using a permitted pre-printed postcard, which meant that it could be sent immediately, bypassing the censors. The letter, written in English at the same time, and required to be brief because the censors were overwhelmed, only finally left the censors' office in Sydney on 30 October, five weeks after it had been written. It contained a mix of urgent mundane practicalities (the *Dunera* internees had been despoiled of most of their clothing on the ship) with more intractable needs, expressed as: 'I wrote already a card. Am here in Australia as internee since 10th September ... If possible please send me two pair of socks, one pair of trousers, pants and shirt. I am very well indeed and would be quite happy if I would know the whereabouts of my whole family.'

Further cards and letters from Paul followed throughout September, October and November, but there was never a response.

There is not much to report from me. The situation is unchanged and the time passes in waiting for news from Olga and from you. Till now I have no letter from anyone.

Nothing new to report. I am still here and am quite well, only I have no letters either from you or from anyone else.

I think that all my letters are beginning with the same sentence: I have no letter from you since I am here and this is I am sure rather a long time. I would be only too glad to receive a few lines from you.

One day passes like the other, dull, no work of any value to do and the worst of all no letters and no books. But never mind, in 50 years it's all the same and nobody will then know anything about our troubles.

Finally, in early December, two letters arrived from Olga, and a few days later, at last a card from Walter. Three months had elapsed. 'Thank heavens yesterday I received your card from October 25th,' Paul wrote. To Lilly a week later, he added: 'I cannot explain how glad I was to receive this letter because I learned of it that all of you are well. I have also already some letters from Olga who also cabled me some money so that I can write sometimes by air mail.' Paul's requests in these letters were for simple things: 'Perhaps it is possible for you, if the postage is not too high, to send me some fiction-books, a small dictionary and perhaps also a chemistry book. If possible direct from the publisher because of the censor,' he wrote. He had initially asked for clothing, a parcel of which was sent from the US, though as it was relatively hot now his need for this had lessened, and he was keen not to overload himself with possessions: 'I am now equipped with the main things and do not want to carry too much on my next journey,' he wrote in January. He continued to wish to study technical chemistry, to keep up his skills: 'Perhaps you could obtain a catalogue of technical chemistry books, especially with regard to fats and waxes.' He was not worried about himself, just sentenced to waiting for news: 'Time passes by reading and learning and waiting for post, this waiting is the hardest work because one never gets accustomed to it.'

This 'next journey' he imagined was to be to the US. Already in his first letter from Hay, Paul showed awareness of the Australian Government policy of refusing to accept the internees for settlement: 'As it seems impossible to remain here I have to go to your country but it will take some time,' he wrote. And in his next letter: 'Perhaps I have to go to your country although I would not like to do it because – you know it already – I always think that Australia is the country where I could work in my special line as lanolin maker.'

There was a double irony, that Paul had, after all, come to Australia, which had consistently been his preferred place of exile, and now that he was there, he was not allowed to stay other than as an internee. Regardless of the British Government's reversal on their internment policy as early as July 1940, the Australian Government was resolutely opposed to doing the same thing. Instead, Australia chose to see itself purely as the custodian of the internees on behalf of the British Government, and unless the internees were returned to Britain, they would have to remain under guard where they were.

Quite apart from a general resistance to foreign immigration, vividly expressed in the shameless White Australia Policy (which restricted non-Anglo-Celtic immigration), the fact that the internees were mostly Jewish did not help their cause. A senior politician in a speech in Melbourne in May 1939 described Jewish immigrants as 'slinking, rat-faced men under 5 foot in height, and with a chest development of about 20 inches', who lived in slums and were prepared to work for a pittance, thereby undercutting local labour. The new prime minister, Robert Menzies, regarded this charge as a serious allegation worthy of immediate investigation. Few politicians in Australia were prepared to take up the case of the internees; it was not a popular cause.

As a result of this policy, Paul had to focus again on getting his application for a US visa in order.

> *On my voyage I lost my notebook and will ask you to send me by airmail all particulars about my affidavit (guarantor, registration number and date etc.). The documents – lying in London, partly at the American Consulate General, partly at the lawyer (of which I can't neither remember the name nor the address but you will know it and therefore I ask you to be so kind as to write it) – have to be transferred to this country. Please write me also the addresses of all our friends (Olga, Paula, Mathilde, Tonie, Martin, Kurt Paul Müller* [Martha's brother], *Nettel* [an exile in Tokyo] *etc.).*

Paul's reconciliation to the idea of going to the US puzzled Paula when she finally had news of his situation: 'Why do you think that Paul will travel to you?' she asked Walter. 'He always wanted originally to go to the Müllers [i.e. Sydney]'. She was unaware of the Australian Government's adamant opposition on resettlement of the internees.

Chapter 8

Vienna

November 1940 to June 1941

In Vienna, in November 1940, the first of a set of new difficulties began to unfold. The family was notified that as part of the policy of forcing Jewish families to live in insalubrious communal apartments, they were shortly to be evicted from the family home in Margaretenstrasse, where conditions had in any case become difficult, especially for Paula's father, Martin, now eighty-two, as there was no longer any heating. But the move from the old family apartment to cramped, shared quarters was stressful: they had to give up their entire library, which had to be 'dispersed', in Paula's words. It had fallen to her to find alternative accommodation in the collective housing to which Jews were now confined, which was not easy: 'We were informed about 3 weeks ago, but after a lot of trekking around and many visits Paula unearthed the new quarters,' wrote her father much later. The new, shared accommodation was much smaller, 'a room and a small room, and the use of a kitchen', with a little balcony, and had to accommodate Paula; her parents; Paul's mother, Mathilde; and Martha Müller.

Paula held the news about the move from Walter until she had found the new place, so as not to worry him. And when they moved in December, she presented it positively: 'We've already moved! Everything went flawlessly! We're already quite well adjusted. The best of it: the stove heats brilliantly. I haven't been so warm in a long time. The lady with whom we're living is very nice and everything is going to be okay.' Hans and Lisl left their dog with the family during the day, as Hans had by now obtained a job at the IKG, and Lisl, being non-Jewish, was permitted to work; the ordinance prohibiting Jews from keeping pets had not yet come into force. 'Tell Olga,' Paula wrote, 'that we're all well, that her mother is fine and that we all live with one another most harmoniously. We've already accustomed ourselves completely to our new milieu and are perfectly content.' Although the rigid censorship of mail meant that the real conditions in Vienna could not be told in the family letters, small details were telling. The mother of a close non-Jewish friend and former hiking companion of Walter's had died: 'The funeral is on December 2nd, and Paula will go to the cemetery and lay a wreath on the grave for us without an inscription and a second with the name "Walter" for you,' wrote his father. (The family name, Haim, would have been too recognisable as Jewish and open to vandalism or worse; the name 'Walter' didn't give much away.)

A few weeks after Paul's arrest, Olga had managed with difficulty to get another live-in job in Bradford as a cook, although she was frustrated that her skills as a paediatrician were still being wasted: 'It is a great pity that I can't find something suitable. I would be so glad if I could work in my line and be useful in one way or another, but still, I am glad that I found something … I don't write very cheerful letters, but you will understand how I feel.' The job at least was not very onerous:

'I haven't too much to work so I feel much better,' she wrote to Paula. By October, the job was getting her down again: 'Everything else is unchanged and rather trying. Today is Yom Kippur – can you imagine how I feel? Absolutely lonely, no friends, nobody I can talk to as a servant. But nevertheless I keep smiling and expect a better future.'

Paula reminded Walter that 'Ollie's birthday will be on 29 November. Please tell her that she must remain healthy for Paul, for her mother, and for me, and that I love her endlessly.' Then, as late as January: 'I am very worried about Olga. She is so alone.' However, Olga's situation had begun to change for the better. In November, she had left her job as a domestic and had moved back to where she had lived previously with Paul: 'I left my post and stay now at Mrs. Hopkinson's. Chances are much better now and I hope I will get a nicer job soon. I am very well and in good spirits.' Finally, by December, the 'nicer job' had at last appeared, in Ilkley, Yorkshire, just north of Bradford:

> *I got a nice job as a Matron in a hostel for sick children. I am very busy & very happy to work a bit in my line. The children are all poor & I am thankful to be allowed to help them as much as I can. I am a quite different person now. A postcard from Paul without date, he is well. What more can I wish for.*

In December, news of Paul's initial card from Hay had reached Paula in Vienna, too. 'I'm happy above all about Paul's card,' she wrote. 'Hopefully a detailed letter from him will also come soon.' (The detailed letter was the one held up with the censor.) On Christmas Eve, she went to have dinner with Hans and Lisl and stayed overnight so that she would not be out on the streets after dark at Christmas, with its heightened risk for a Jewish woman.

In January, it was the anniversary of Alice's death. 'Yesterday it was a year that our very dear, good Alice left,' wrote Paula's father. 'On the previous day (Sunday) Paula and Hansi went to her grave in the morning and Mama and Hans in the afternoon even though the entire cemetery lay deep in snow. It was cold and very windy and unfortunately I could not go out to her.' Paula reported that he remained in good health: 'Papa is quite old and in this year's winter didn't have a cold once, thank God. No one here believes that he's already 82.' Mail continued to be an issue – the family could no longer afford to send airmail letters, and instead had to rely on the slower surface mail. Walter's most recent letter was already two months old.

Their settlement in the new shared apartment was short-lived. In mid-January they were all were forced to move again. The letters to Walter from his father and from Paula simply informed him, without comment or complaint. The mute reporting was a sign of their helplessness as the pressure built. And, indeed, the situation in Vienna was becoming more and more desperate, as large-scale transports to the ghettos of the east, such as Lodz, Opole, Lublin and other places, had recommenced in February 1941. Each weekly transport was of 1000 people. Initially, letters came back to Vienna from those transported, detailing conditions that were ghetto-like, but not so far totally lethal, like the extermination camps. This soon changed: reports of hunger, cold and hard labour began to arrive, with requests for food, clothing and blankets, but the sending of relief packages was soon banned. People learnt with fear of the system for the round-up of deportees. A postcard arrived from Eichmann's office, informing the recipient that they needed to report to a collection point or *Sammellager* (mostly former institutional buildings in the 2nd district) on a certain date in preparation for deportation. They were permitted to bring only 50 kilograms of luggage with them. A typical card read:

Central Office for Jewish Emigration

Eugenstrasse 22, Vienna 4

10th October, 1941

You are to present yourself on 19 Oct. 1941 at 3 p.m. with your dependants and hand luggage weighing a maximum of 50 kg per person at the school at Kleine Sperlgasse 2a, Vienna 2.

In case of non-appearance, you will be brought before the police.

The Head of the Central Office for Jewish Emigration

People became paralysed with fear. As Elizabeth Welt Trahan, a survivor who was sixteen at the time, wrote later:

> People went about their business as if nothing were wrong. At most they would answer unemotionally – 'No, not yet' or 'Yes, I have. My bag is packed and I am ready.' Every day revolved around one excruciating moment – the arrival of the mailman. If he left without delivering a summons, you heaved a sigh of relief knowing that life could go on as usual for another day.

Transport 5 had left Vienna on 12 March 1941.

While people were waiting to be collected for the sixth transport, a rumour spread with lightning speed: the transports were called off. At first we didn't believe it, but soon the Community office confirmed the good news ... The reason for the cessation of transports was ... the need to transport troops to Bulgaria. The good news was celebrated as if it were Sylvester – New Year's Eve. Strangers were hugging and kissing in the street, offering to share their meals, their precious cup of coffee. Tears flowed freely, smiles were ecstatic. The worst was over and normal life could be resumed.

But this was just an illusion: the transports were to resume in the autumn, until virtually the whole Jewish population had been deported by late 1942.

As the inexorable threat to the safety of Paula's household grew, the possibility of somehow getting a visa to the US, or anywhere, became more and more urgent. News continued to arrive from family and friends exiled abroad, in Tokyo, in Rio, in Manila, where mail services with Vienna still existed. News of the success of exiles in America was particularly encouraging, as a model for Walter, still struggling to find decent work, but also as a potential network of contacts in the endless search for ways of getting to the US. Throughout January, February, March and April, Paula reminded Walter constantly of the urgency of obtaining affidavits and the accompanying documentation needed if they were to have any hope of leaving: 'Do what you can for Paul to be able to send for his wife and his mother, and soon – it's crucial for them both ... If you can find an affidavit for anyone in the family, telegraph it immediately. You'll leave no stone unturned, I'm sure of that.' She also continued to press Walter for help with the additional paperwork she needed herself for the affidavit he had obtained for her. 'Tell me, Bobbi, the supporting materials for my affidavit are not to be had at all? I think I'll need them, even if I've got a bad quota number,' she wrote. Alternatively, she asked, could she replace Alice on the affidavits Hans had already obtained, as Paul had discussed with him a year earlier in relation to Olga?

In addition to the US, Paula had still not entirely given up hope of Paul getting her to Australia, with the help of Martha's brother-in-law in Sydney:

> *I am so happy that we've now again got regular news from you and Paul. You'll know where Bela is. He is the brother-in-law of Martha Müller, with whom their mother lives. He's called Bela Gertler. Paul and he are already in touch with Olga. He's also taken steps to have Paul and me come to him.*

In addition to the endless visa issues, there was also the issue of how to pay for the ship's tickets – the family's assets had been taken from them, and work was forbidden: 'Can Ollie possibly come up with ship's tickets if my affidavit is ever finalized?' Paula asked Walter. Her brother Hans faced the same dilemma: 'Without ship's tickets you can't travel, and I've got no ship's tickets,' he wrote. 'You can perhaps get tickets for December 1941 or January 1942, but they're not available without a correspondingly high payment of dollars, and as luck would have it, I have no money, so this is out of the question.'

But her hopes that Paul might get a US visa were dashed when Walter received a letter in February from the Secretary of the Sephardic Refugee Committee. 'With reference to obtaining a renewal of the affidavit for your brother-in-law I regret to inform you that Mr. Katzner died the day after your wife came to see me regarding the matter. It is therefore impossible to obtain a renewal of Mr. Katzner's affidavit.'

'The death of Mr. Katzner leaves everything cold, the more so because we didn't know anything of him or of his life,' Hans wrote. And now they would have to begin again the exhausting process of finding someone else who would act as a guarantor and swear an affidavit of support. Paul was not concerned for himself with this news, but for those left behind in Vienna: 'Do not worry about me and about Mr. Katzner. I am perfectly all right. Please tell me: is there no possibility to do anything for Paula, Lilly's parents, Tonie, Martin and Mathilde? As far as I know things do not seem to be pleasant for them.' Despite this serious setback, a faint hope for Paula remained alive: 'Mr. Hendricks [a wealthy member of the New York City Sephardic community] telegraphed me that he has extended his affidavit for Paula,' Hans wrote. 'Hopefully the papers will come also and she will be able to use them.'

Hopefully, indeed. But miracles did happen: Lilly's parents, the Neuhauses, and Walter's parents-in-law, in early 1941, were successful in their second attempt to get a US visa and were busy preparing to depart. They left via train to Berlin from Vienna's Ostbahnhof on the evening of 17 March, from there travelling overland via Moscow, Inner Mongolia, Manchuria and on to Kobe in Japan, before getting a ship across the Pacific to Seattle, and from there to New York. An itinerary made available by the IKG, a phone call from Berlin and a series of postcards allowed the family to anxiously trace their long and difficult journey: 'The Neuhaus parents are already very far away, we follow their journey on the map that the emigrants receive and that we have also,' Paula and Walter's mother, Tonie, wrote. Lilly's maternal grandmother, Omama, was left behind, in the old people's home in Seegasse, where she was visited by Tonie and Paula. Tonie wrote to Walter about the departure:

> *I am very sick again and very sad that they aren't here any longer, and I always believed until the last moment that I would be very happy that they were travelling to you, and that you would be glad and happy about that, and now I sit here and cry. But when with God's help they finally really are with you, I will be overwhelmed and will be able to be happy about it with you. Yesterday I found Omama, too, still very sad and we cried together, nothing else is possible, then we were a little bit happier, and when I left we had already discussed and talked about our own trip to you.*

Paula was determined to somehow take her parents to the US. She wrote to Walter, 'I'm confident that you have considered every possibility; hopefully you'll be successful in bringing everyone there … If Paul manages to get to you, it will perhaps be easier to meet the requirements for the mothers.' Her father's health was deteriorating: 'He is still bedridden, today significantly better, but this changes three times a day. It seems to stem from vascular cramps, very painful, afterwards always inevitably great weakness,' reported Hans. Martin managed to recover from this immediate crisis: 'Today I'm glad to tell you that Papa, thank God, is significantly better. A decisive improvement has taken place in the last few days … It was very serious this time and has never lasted this long! Mama was very busy with his care, which was a huge amount of work for her.' The implications for the possibility of her father travelling to the United States were clear. Censorship required Paula to refer to her parents as 'Paul's in-laws': 'To speak plainly, for his father-in-law such a journey to you is out of the question now, except in summer, but even then it would be questionable whether he could handle the trip. But we must also think hard about his mother-in-law.'

All hope of getting to the US was finally extinguished in June 1941, when the US State Department issued a new regulation denying a visa to anyone who had relatives in Axis-occupied territory. Walter had continued to reach out to organisations about possible emigration for Paul to the US. On 8 July 1941, he wrote to the Board of National Missions of the Presbyterian Church in the U.S.A. asking about an affidavit of support for him. The Board responded two days later:

> I note what you write with regard to the need of an affidavit for Mr Kurz, but am afraid that even with an affidavit there is no prospect at present for him to secure the necessary immigration quota visa to come to the States.
>
> You, of course, know of the new regulation with regard to immigration to America. These are rather drastic and make it well-nigh impossible for any interned individual to come to the States, at least not while the war is on. I am sorry that the situation is thus and that as a result we can hold out little hope to help you in facilitating your brother-in-law's immigration.

It was thus now virtually impossible to get a visa. This was a blow for Paul, but an even worse blow for Paula and her family. The path to the United States was finally, definitively closed.

Chapter 9

Vienna: The Last Letters

June to December 1941

For some time, Paula had been considering opportunities for employment as a nurse with the IKG, in whose office her brother Hans was employed as a cashier. She had been unable to continue her work as a bookkeeper/auditor in her father's firm since Jewish businesses had been closed following the Anschluss. Even before Olga's departure later in the same year, Paula had accompanied her and her colleague Dr Brügel on their clinical rounds, over the course of an entire year. Like Olga, Paula's close friend Martha Müller had lost her job as paediatrician in the Jewish children's hospital at that time. However, the Nazi authorities had put new arrangements in place for the management of an entirely segregated set of institutions for the immediate health and welfare needs of the Jewish community while the process of deportation was underway. This was all to be managed by the IKG, under the oversight of the Nazis.

Martha was permitted to work in such an institution, and by November 1939 had a position in the children's home for Jewish children. This had given Paula an idea: 'I would be happy if I got something, too,' she had written at the time. In September 1940, an option for possible employment emerged: 'It's possible that I'll also be taken on in the home where Martha Müller works. I'll find out this week.' The immediate start of her nursing career was facilitated by the brother of a woman in the Jewish communal apartment with whom Paula and the family were living: 'Her brother I thank for my entire nursing career!' she wrote.

The IKG had begun to establish several temporary old people's homes, to cater for the needs of elderly Jewish people whose younger relatives had emigrated but who themselves were unable to obtain visas because of their age. In March 1941, Paula started work as a nurse in one of these. 'Since Monday I am a nurse in the home where Uncle Gustl's mother-in-law lives,' she wrote. 'It is a good position. I already have the kit. Now we are three: Olli, Martha and I in the same profession.' Three weeks later she wrote from night duty: 'I am also very happy with my new profession. I would never have thought earlier that I would have any. Just think, Olli and I both go about now "in uniform". How wonderful it would be for me if I could work under her'.

Paula's new role involved completing the nursing training provided by the IKG. Since the middle of 1938, the IKG had been running training courses for nurses, replacing the non-Jewish staff, who were no longer permitted contact with Jewish patients. She attended lectures almost daily at the main home in Seegasse, where Omama was living, and in June moved to work there. In September 1941, she took her nursing examinations, which she passed with flying colours, although she felt she had had an unfair advantage because of her previous experience with Olga and her colleague Brügel. 'There isn't much to say about the test, it was child's play,' she wrote.

> *And most of the poor candidates were at a bit of a disadvantage because of their rather basic family backgrounds and otherwise a bit behind, so that it really was no feat to be among the best. For me, I was already familiar with so many medical things from the year-long rotation with Brügel and Olli, about which most of them could have no concept even after the most zealous study. I am happy about my profession and it suits me and that it is demanding is a true blessing for me.*

At the same time, however, a new blow occurred: Martin, whose health had given cause for concern for several months, died in the summer of 1941. Paula wrote:

> *I'm sitting in the room in which he felt so comfortable, his fat, brown armchair sits in the sun – but empty. It's awful how much we miss him. I'm writing with his fountain pen, I've taken over his closet, and I know that he'd only be too happy about that. He would also have been happy about my test, which I passed "with honours". He wouldn't have expected anything else from me. He always had a good opinion of me … And he loved you both a lot and had a great respect for "little Lilly". He always admired decent, straightforward people who, in his opinion, knew how to bear difficulties, too.'*

Tonie expressed her grief to her son, and her stoical acceptance:

> *I'm happy whenever someone comes, it always distracts one somewhat from one's troubles, I can't really say troubles but thoughts, so no, the wound is still very fresh, if you look around the room and he's not here anymore, but everything reminds me of him, and through that he still lives with us, but it's a sad substitute. But it can't be changed.*

I'd like to have your letter by now and see from it, Walter, that you don't rebel against what has happened but rather say to yourself that parents must die some time. That this point in time always comes too early is understandable, but can't be changed.

On 1 September 1941, it was decreed that Jews were required to wear the yellow star. Elizabeth Welt Trahan, who was protected for the time being by her Romanian nationality, was not required to wear it, and was able to move about freely, not obviously identifiable as Jewish. One day she decided to see what difference it would make if she wore it.

One time my friend Ditha forgot her jacket at my place. For a while I studied its bright yellow star, then I put it on and went out … I wanted to know what it felt like – perhaps I also wanted in some minor way to make amends for my privileged status. It was an unnerving experience. I may have imagined it, but it seemed to me that everybody was either staring at me as if I were a freak, or looking away deliberately, pretending that I didn't exist … I stopped at a shop window, not to glance at its display but because I was startled to see my reflection wearing a star. As if I as a non-Jew was seeing a Jew for the first time, and also seeing myself for the first time as a Jew. Then I noticed a saleslady inside motioning to me to move on … In my hurry to get home I forgot to cover the star. I rushed upstairs in a sweat and tore off the jacket. I felt like an escaped convict, subhuman, branded. How could my friends stand it, how could they live in this city and among these people day after day, and not lose their self-respect or become violent?

Vienna: The Last Letters

Because of censorship, and the need to reassure Walter, such increasingly desperate circumstances of life were not communicated in letters to him, apart from an occasional hint.

Paul remained close to Paula's heart. At least now she knew where he was and received news of him from time to time via the Müllers in Australia: 'Martha today received a somewhat stale letter from her mother in which she writes that she often has news from Padli [a nickname for Paul], and that she wants to visit him.' By coincidence, one of the people Paula and her family were now living with was the best friend of another *Dunera* internee, Dr Julius Schwarcz. 'His telephone number is 56-5-62 (Paul I believe is 57-492?),' she wrote, giving their internment numbers as their telephone numbers, because of the censorship of letters. She complained again to Walter that he communicated insufficiently about Paul: 'In three days it will be Padli's birthday. The third without me. How many more? I hope that you tell Padli more about us than you tell me about him. Details specifically.'

Later that month, she wrote: 'Today I will go to sleep very soon. I had two night shifts one after the other. Every day, when I come off the shift, I tell Paul in spirit about everything that the day brought me. Unfortunately, only in spirit, and if I am sometimes at a loss, no one answers me. A good "training" to cope with everything.'

This was her last letter to Walter. In October the mass deportations resumed. In December, United States entered the war following the attack on Pearl Harbor, which meant that mail services with the Reich ended. All communication from Paula to Walter now ceased.

Chapter 10

Tatura; Melbourne
May 1941 to May 1943; 1943 to 1945

What to do with the internees who had been sent to Australia from Britain remained a problem, given the adamant refusal of the Australian Government to allow them settled status. In March 1941, Major Julian Layton, who had been active in the resettlement of refugees in Britain, was sent out as the representative of the British Home Secretary to investigate the conditions of the internees and to conduct discussions with the Australian Government about their return to Britain.

On arrival in Hay, Layton was concerned about the inhospitable climatic conditions there. Perhaps because of this, but also due to the concern of pressure on the facilities, with the anticipated arrival of more internees and prisoners of war, a decision was made to transfer the *Dunera* internees to a site in northern Victoria, where camps already existed. Paul left Hay on 19 May and arrived at Tatura, some 250 kilometres to the south, the following day. Several camps had been built on requisitioned agricultural land in an irrigation area a few kilometres from Tatura, the nearest small town. The land around was relatively flat, with low rolling hills, extending for miles in all directions. A number of camps were used to house the *Dunera* internees, one of whom, a Jesuit priest, recalled the journey from Hay to Tatura and his first impressions there:

> The trip to Tatura was quite rapid: over the Murrumbidgee River, through endless plains, past enormous wheat fields and forests of light eucalyptus trees, amongst which you could spot every now and then a homestead, towards Camp 2 … We saw signs of life only seldom, a solitary farmer driving his tractor, flocks of sheep, a mob of kangaroos or emus. The first thing that struck us about the new camp was the complete change of scenery and climate. The camp was situated in a lonely, rolling landscape. On the left shone the surface of a dam, surrounded by silent pine forests. In front of us on the right, there was more pastureland studded with big eucalyptus trees. An irrigation channel some distance away brought water from the lake to the fruit plantations in the Shepparton district, and continued on further to the Goulburn River.

'As you will see on the new address we have moved to a new camp,' Paul wrote shortly after arriving. 'It is very nice here. I am perfectly all right. Nothing to worry about me.' There were accommodation huts, shared toilets and ablution facilities, a kitchen, administration buildings and some recreation facilities; the internees soon created a garden. The boundary was surrounded by barbed wire. Bob Vogel, Paul's young campmate, wrote years later: 'In Tatura, life went on much the same as it did in Hay, but being a fruit-picking area, we had working parties going out fruit picking. One guard to every fifty or so internees that went out on working parties. And life was generally easier. We had all sorts of classes, lectures, and actually got papers from the universities.' (Not all internees shared this view; many, in fact, preferred Hay, for various reasons.)

Paul was generally uncomplaining about his immediate circumstances in the camp – that was not the real issue: 'Time passes by in reading and learning and now and then a little bit working', although two years into his internment he made one mordant remark about the fact that Churchill had acknowledged that Britain's internment policy in 1940 had been a 'mistake': 'I would like to be with you now and do something no matter what to give my little share in an honest way. But instead I am condemned to stay here idle and to rust because of a little mistake'. To keep his skills up to date in order to secure employment and hence possible release, he continued to request books on the 'chemical technology of oils, fats and waxes'. 'I am quite o.k. Learning, reading, waiting. As to your question: The climate here isn't bad at all. Hot days occur everywhere and when I work I don't feel it. But now winter starts here and we get also quite cold days,' he wrote.

A year after moving to Tatura: 'On the whole I am all-right. I do a bit of reading and learning but it is not much and nevertheless somehow time goes by.' And a further year later: 'As to me I have not much to tell. I am still working at our vegetable garden. This keeps me quite occupied and fit too.' Martha Müller's family in Sydney were a support: 'From Irma [Martha's mother] I had a parcel with a nice cake and from Bela [Martha's brother-in-law] I received a letter. You see I am well looked after by our friends.'

Letters were important to him in his endless Godot-like waiting. Paul wrote fortnightly to Walter: 'If it is possible please do not stop writing, at least do write once a month.' And to Lilly: 'Although I had some cards of Walter of a later date, (which I confirmed already a fortnight ago) I would very much like to receive more mail from you or from him'. He was in regular contact with Olga, who in early 1942 had found a job in a children's hospital in south London. Another of Paul's young campmates at Tatura, Walter Foster, then a teenager, years later recalled life there:

> I made several good friends with whom I walked endlessly around the perimeter wire probing our many personal problems and worries, discussing the course of the war as reflected in the newspapers, rehearsing our hopes for the future, and trying to recall the ever more receding world outside the wire ... There was Paul Kurz, 20 years my senior and a doctor of chemistry; he taught me carpentry in the workshop he had established for himself in Tatura Camp, he also tried to teach me – much less successfully – his philosophy to take life as it comes and to make the best of things one is not able to change.

In one of Paul's characteristically brief letters from Tatura ('I always start to write a letter and then I see a post-card would have done it, as there is nothing new to tell') he made explicit this philosophy:

> *Believe me it is absolutely useless to make any plans for the future. It always comes otherwise than one thinks. All events happen as they are forced to happen and it is good luck that we never know how they are forced to happen. Please do me a favour: do not worry anymore about my future because there won't be any. Thank heavens you did not make those experiences I did but I have to ask you as not to build*

your fairy-castles too high. It does not hurt so much if one falls only from a modest height. I am really all-right as far as this is possible.

Paul's main preoccupation, of course, was what was happening to Paula and his mother in Vienna, news of whom was increasingly difficult to come by, now that the US declaration of war with Germany in December 1941 meant the cessation of the mail service between the two countries: Walter could no longer be a conduit. All communication would have to be through other indirect channels, via neutral countries and networks of contacts. 'The main task is, patience, and hope, for seeing you all again. I wrote already four times to Paula but till now I got no answer. Things don't look very bright for them,' he wrote in March 1942. A month later: 'From Tonie, I have no news since a very long time'. Later that month, some news did come, indirectly as always: 'Have you had any news from Tonie. I learned from Bela that he had a letter from Martha who is living with Tonie. They are all right.' In July: 'Till to now I have no reply from Tonie. One thing more to wait for.' In September of 1942: 'I also can't get any reply on my different letters to Paula. This month I will try to write through the Red Cross. It is now more than one year I last heard from her, and that is not very easy to bear. But in a fifty years' time, it is all the same.'

Paul's last news of Paula was some time in 1943, probably early in the year. To a question in the Report on Application for Naturalization in 1944, 'Are the particulars stated regarding his wife correct?' Paul answered: 'Yes. When last heard of in 1943, she was then in Vienna.' News had been coming in for some time of the fate of deportees to Poland. In April 1943, in response to a suggestion from Paul, Walter attempted to contact the Swedish Red Cross in Stockholm, but the letter was opened and then returned to him marked 'Returned to

Sender by Censor'. In the letter Walter asked whether it was possible to contact his family, specifically his mother, Tonie; his brother, Hans; Paula; and Paul's mother, Mathilde: 'Will you, please, have the great kindness to inform me whether there is any possibility to contact my family, formerly in Vienna, Austria, now most probably brought to Poland. I did not hear from them since November 1941.'

Paul responded to the news that Walter had made this inquiry (but not yet perhaps that his letter had been returned) with pessimism about its likely outcome. The gravity of his tone, and the remark that 'in the meantime all has changed', suggested that Paul had, by now, fully absorbed the impact of the news reports of the deportations and the extermination camps. 'On June 28th, I received your letter of May 16th,' he wrote.

> *I appreciate it the more as it is written in plain language, facts without circumscription. I have nothing to add. You are absolutely right in saying I must wait till to a definite proof. I do not think you will get any information neither through the Red Cross nor through the Society of Friends. In my first letter I wrote to you from this town I still was somehow more hopeful and therefore I suggested the Swedish Red Cross but in the meantime everything has changed.*

And, indeed, there was no more news. An official letter in October 1944 in connection with Paul's application for Australian Permanent Resident status merely stated: 'If his wife is alive after the cessation of hostilities in Europe, he will make an application for her admission to Australia.'

Despite the Australian Government's hard-line stance about only releasing the internees on condition that they were being returned to England, a slow trickle of releases was allowed. In some cases, it was because individuals were considered valuable to the war effort; in others, the result of lobbying efforts on behalf of Christian internees by Christian groups; in yet others, the opportunity for immigration to Palestine arranged by Zionist groups. One avenue was release to service in military units, initially to the Pioneer Corps of the British Army, followed in 1942 by the establishment of a unit in the Australian Army in which internees could volunteer to serve on tasks such as loading and unloading ships, or agricultural labour, although it meant that freedom would probably only come after demobilisation at the end of the war, which for many turned out to be as late as 1946. (This was by no means true for all: many were demobbed within a year or two of enlisting.)

Many, particularly younger internees, chose the option of volunteering for this army unit. Others, including Paul, did not, for a number of possible reasons. One rather unlikely explanation is that those with family in Germany and the former Austria, such as Paul, may have felt concerned that news that they had enlisted in the enemy army would jeopardise their safety, such as it was, although the possibility of this news reaching the Reich was minimal. The thought of an uncertain demobilisation date was a disincentive to volunteering. Paul was one of the older internees – he was forty-one in 1942 – which may have been a factor in his reluctance to volunteer for army work. There was also the possibility of being allowed to be released to work in an industry that was seen as useful to the nation at war, and he had kept his professional knowledge and skills alive and up to date, as far as possible.

In March 1943, nearly three years after his arrest in Bradford, Paul was finally allowed to leave. He was one of the last to be released from Tatura into civilian life: by the time of his release only 200 internees remained in Camp 2. He moved to Melbourne, took a room in a house in Armadale owned by a landlord with the resonant name of Friederich Schiller, from Vienna, and took up a job in a company called Lanoline Products at the Yarra Falls Mills, which produced wool and silk textiles, in Abbotsford, Melbourne. He continued to wait. And wait. And wait. For a further two years, until the war in Europe finally ended in May 1945.

In early June he wrote to Walter: 'I have your letter of April 7th in which you informed me about your trying to contact Vienna through your Red Cross. Already in my last letter I told you that I did the same and I'll do it again this month. There is nothing I could report.' And towards the end of June: 'There is nothing I could tell about me. One day like the other. Waiting for miracles is my pastime.'

Chapter 11

Vienna: After the Letters Stopped

January 1942 to early 1943

Miracles in Vienna were few and far between. What had happened to Paula had to be inferred from sources such as others' letters, memoirs, historical accounts and archival records, in the absence of communication from her. Large-scale deportations rolled relentlessly on throughout 1942; smaller deportations continued irregularly thereafter. Conditions became more and more oppressive by the month for the remaining Jews in Vienna. Food rations became more restricted, Jews were forbidden to buy foodstuffs such as meat, eggs, milk and flour, and buildings needed to indicate on the outside that there were Jewish occupants inside. There were random raids and house-to-house searches; neighbours often reported minor infringements of regulations to the SS and arrests were frequent.

In February 1942, the household of Paula, Tonie, Mathilde and Martha Müller, after fourteen months in a communal apartment in the 4th district, was moved to another in the 2nd district, where the surviving Jewish population was increasingly concentrated. Through a terrible

Vienna: After the Letters Stopped

irony, the *Judenhaus* (building in which Jews were concentrated) to which they were moved at the end of February 1942 was at Novaragasse 40, across the street from the apartment at Novaragasse 39, where Mathilde Kurz had lived and raised her children, where Ignaz Kurz had operated a grocery store and where Paul had grown up. Their neighbour, at Novaragasse 41, was Dr Paul Klaar, whose position involved making the agonising decision of whether people were healthy enough to be transported – a position from which he could not save anyone's life, although he might be able to delay their deportation; he was Paula's boss for a short time. The Riesenrad (giant Ferris wheel, owned by a Jewish businessman before the Anschluss, then 'Aryanised') loomed at the end of the street.

Slowly, relentlessly, the deportation program reached Paula and her family. From November 1941, the system of sending postcards from the Central Office for Jewish Emigration summoning people to report for deportation was replaced by a more violent system, in response to the failure of individuals to report to the collection camps (*Sammellager*) at the appointed time and place. Now, SS officers would arrive at the apartment of the deportee, who was given two hours to pack, the street sometimes having been closed off and guards located outside the building. The SS men were accompanied by a Jewish *Ordner* or *Ausheber* (marshall) from the IKG, whose job ostensibly was to help people pack, but actually it was to prevent them from escaping between the departure of the SS officers and the arrival of the trucks to pick up the luggage. Help with the luggage was provided by a *Gepäckträger* (baggage handler), also provided by the IKG, who loaded the packed bags, unloaded them at the *Sammellager*, and loaded them again for the deportation train. There were about 15 to 20 *Gepäckträger* and about a hundred *Ordner*, all of whom were themselves ultimately deported and murdered.

The deportee was then accompanied to the *Sammellager*. The conditions there were extremely crowded and unhygienic; a person might be held there for several days. Finally, an assessment was made by Anton Brunner, the officer responsible for the *Sammellager*, and his SS men. This process was known as *Kommissionierung* ('commissioning'), a ritual of humiliation that was deeply feared, as it was where final decisions would be made as to 'dismissal', 'deferment' or 'deportation' (called 'evacuation'). Those who were considered 'fully Jewish' usually had no chance of escaping deportation to ghettoes and extermination camps in Poland or to other sites in the east, or, from June 1942 for older deportees, to Theresienstadt in Bohemia, which acted as a stepping stone to the death camps. Those deported to Theresienstadt rather than to the east included the elderly, culturally prominent individuals, people with political positions, employees of the IKG and its successor, the *Ältestenrat* (Council of Elders), and doctors and nurses from Jewish hospitals, most of which were being shut down and their patients also transferred to Theresienstadt.

A waiver of assets had to be signed, and all valuables and cash handed over. Documents had to be produced; passports, birth certificates and other precious paperwork, such as affidavits, were often torn up in front of the internee and the identity card stamped 'evacuated'. Only those who were protected by a non-Jewish spouse or parent, had foreign citizenship or were among the employees of the IKG and their immediate dependants, could hope for 'deferment'. But even for those, deferment was temporary; deportations of these people continued until the end of the war.

The deportations first impacted Paula's family in August 1942. For several years she had been visiting Omama and writing reports of the visits to Walter; Omama was not a blood relative, but the Haim and Neuhaus families had become very close. The aged care home at

Vienna: After the Letters Stopped

Seegasse was being systematically emptied and would soon be handed over to the SS. Omama was rounded up with 155 other home residents and held for a time in a *Sammellager* in the 2nd district. Paula must have been aware of this but could do nothing; she was helpless. On 27 August 1942, Omama was taken as part of Transport 38 to the Aspang railway station in Vienna, en route to Theresienstadt. A survivor of a deportation shortly afterwards described the process:

> The roundup was carried out late at night ... when I was brought to the assembly point in the 2nd District, the building was already packed full. When the order came to prepare for evacuation on September 24th, each of us was forced to pass before the Gestapo with his or her backpack or suitcase. We were then loaded onto trucks; to me – as a meat trader – this image of the evacuation resembled the transportation of beef to the abattoir in Vienna. The people of Vienna couldn't care less what happened to the Jews ... We arrived in Theresienstadt the following day at about noon. As we alighted from the train, we already had the first dead ... who hadn't survived the transport. We had to alight at the station in Bohusovice [Bauschowitz], since there was still no direct train to Theresienstadt.

On arrival, Omama was immediately admitted to the hospital of the barracks to which she had been assigned, but the trauma of her removal was too much for her and she died less than a fortnight later. She was eighty-two.

A similarly traumatic separation involved Paula's closest friend, Martha Müller. At some time after March 1942, Martha was moved from the crowded accommodation she was sharing with Paula, her mother and Paul's mother in Novaragasse, to the site of the Jewish children's home and day care centre on Mohapelgasse, where she was employed. Although she was a specialist doctor (*Facharztin*), she was now only allowed the title of *(Fach)krankenbehandlerin* ((Specialist) treater of the sick). When the fourteen children remaining in Mohapelgasse were deported to Theresienstadt, she accompanied them, whether by choice or by compulsion is not clear. She left Vienna on Transport 42 on 24 September, the eleventh transport from Vienna to Theresienstadt. Several accounts exist of the experience of people on this transport. One witness reported:

> On the night of September 22, a Jewish man arrived at my apartment ... in order to take me away ... Despite my protests, I was taken to the assembly camp ... SS personnel confiscated our birth certificates and left us only with our identity cards after imprinting them with the stamp 'Relocated to Theresienstadt'. Before being taken away, all the women and men were forced to have their hair cut. The first trucks arrived at nine in the morning to collect us from the transit camp and the last ones arrived at 2:30 in the afternoon. We were forced to stand upright in the open trucks, while people in the crowded streets jeered at us as we were driven past. We were taken to Aspang station ... where we received the paper bag with our food for the journey. But there was nothing to drink. The SS men locked the doors and some of them travelled on the engine. The windows had to be kept closed and we were forbidden to look outside. Our transport, the eleventh from Vienna to Theresienstadt, departed at about five in the afternoon on Tuesday ... The train travelled all night. When I looked out of the window at ten thirty in the morning,

> despite being forbidden from doing so, I recognised Prague. We continued to travel at great speed and arrived in the afternoon at Bohusovice, where we had to alight. The transport consisted of old people and a medical team. On the station platform we were awaited by camp commandant Seidl, a number of SS men, and two or three members of the Czech gendarmerie ... We were forced to walk to Theresienstadt.

Martha survived for two years in Theresienstadt, working as a paediatrician, before she was deported to Auschwitz in October 1944 and murdered there in one of the last groups to suffer death in the gas chambers. She was thirty-eight.

The next deportation, three weeks later, on 9 October 1942, of Paul's mother, Mathilde Kurz, with whom Paula and her mother Tonie were living, involved the forced removal from their own shared apartment, right in front of their eyes, so to speak. As an employee of the IKG, Paula was unable to extend the temporary protection she had to Paul's mother, who was only her mother-in-law, not a direct dependant like her own mother. Mathilde was taken to the main *Sammellager* at Kleine Sperlgasse. A witness described the conditions there:

> The Sammellager at Sperlgasse used to be a school; the school rooms had been cleared out. People lay on mattresses, one next to the other, with only as much space as the size of the mattress. People were not given anything to cover themselves with. That was terrible in winter, people were freezing, the rooms were not heated.

There were inadequate washing or toilet facilities, and the place was filthy, with vermin.

Paul's mother was deported to Theresienstadt on Transport 45. One of the deportees, who survived, recalled:

> From Sperlgasse, the assembly site for deportees destined for Theresienstadt, we were taken by bus to the train station, where we were made to stand like animals. [On our way] to the station, we were accompanied by rabble that gradually filled every street corner in Vienna, with loud cries of 'Die Jew'. At ten o'clock at night we were loaded on to horse trucks and arrived the following morning at 10 am at Bauschowitz. There was no direct rail line to Theresienstadt.

In Theresienstadt, Paul's mother was put into a barracks near her widowed younger sister, Anna, who had been deported from their hometown in Moravia four months earlier. The awareness of each sister's suffering must have been incredibly distressing. But they were finally put in the same room in the barracks, and being together would have been a comfort. The conditions for elderly people were particularly bad: they were put in the upper storeys of barracks buildings (Theresienstadt had been a military fortress during the Habsburg rule) which were cold and filthy. Paul's mother managed to survive in Theresienstadt for five months, before succumbing in the main hospital during an operation for an enlarged kidney. While there were numerous doctors in Theresienstadt, the conditions and equipment in the hospital were primitive. She died on 24 February 1943. She was sixty-eight. Anna was deported to Auschwitz in late December 1943, where she was murdered. She was sixty-four.

By October 1942, the vast number of those Jews who had been unable to find a way to leave Vienna had been deported: only 5000 of

Vienna: After the Letters Stopped

those counted as Jewish under the Nuremberg Laws were spared for the time being. Of these, about 4000, or 80 per cent, were protected by marriage to or a dependent of a non-Jewish person. Hans was one of them. Unlike many other non-Jewish people, Lisl did not abandon her husband, even though she and Hans were forced into crowded communal housing in the 2nd district reserved for Jews, and subject to many restrictions, including reduced food rations. Non-Jewish spouses were also subject to intense social pressure to abandon their partners. Many of those given temporary protection from deportation in this way did not themselves identify as Jewish, although they were so classified under the Nuremberg Laws, their families having long since converted to Christianity in many cases or having largely cut themselves off from even secular Jewish life.

The Nazi authorities had the intention of deporting even these remaining 4000 but held off for fear of public unrest from the non-Jewish relatives of the individuals concerned; in fact, close to the end of the war, the order was given for their deportation, and it was carried out in other cities in the Reich, but not in Vienna. The rest, about 1000 people, were 'full Jews', a mixture of employees of the *Ältestenrat* (Council of Elders, the successor to the IKG) and their dependents, who were also given temporary protection from deportation: these included Paula and her mother, but this protection could be revoked at any moment. Hans was also employed by the *Ältestenrat*, as a cashier, but was principally protected by his marriage. The end of the deportations meant that many of the institutions previously operated by the IKG were no longer needed, including the many aged care homes, whose residents and their carers had been deported. Still, for the time being the need to segregate those protected from deportation meant that a number of new institutions were required, most concentrated in the

2nd district. Paula was employed in the *Altersheim* (aged care home) at Malzgasse 7, a former school building.

Paula's life as a nurse in the aged care home was demanding, as the hours were punishing (up to seventy-five hours a week) with frequent night duty and twenty-four-hour shifts. The Gestapo would arrive without warning to ensure the staff were wearing the Jewish star on the aprons of their uniform. The residents were, for the most part, those with a non-Jewish close family member. These employees of the IKG and its successor were particularly targeted by the Gestapo. A nurse at the hospital across the road at Malzgasse 16 reported:

> In 1943, many people from the IKG were deported on Transports. For example, we had a nurse who lived with her parents. After she was employed in the hospital, nothing happened to her parents until 1943. Then they said: 'What? Three full Jews? That's too many!' So they took the parents; and the daughter either went with them voluntarily, or they took her too.

Paula and her mother were moved to Lazenhof 2 in the 1st district, another building managed by the Jewish community, in March 1943. There were four women to a room. The building was just across from the Danube Canal separating the 2nd and 1st districts, and perilously close to the notorious headquarters of the Gestapo in the former Hotel Metropole at Morzinplatz, only 200 metres away. Paula would have lived in a permanent state of fear of being deported, her suitcase packed ready to avoid the stress and emotional chaos of trying to pack without notice when the SS men arrived. Her fellow nurses, even if they were 'half-Jews' (having only one Jewish parent), testified to this fear: 'Every time they rang the doorbell, you had to expect they were coming to get

Vienna: After the Letters Stopped

you. The famous suitcase packed ready for the deportation stood in my room for months.' This was echoed by a second nurse: 'I was afraid of deportation all the time, and my suitcase was always packed. When I needed a blouse, I took one out and put the other in. You were never safe, there was no question of that.' And a third: 'We knew from the SS and the SA that they were thinking of making Vienna *judenrein* [cleansed of Jews] and that we were all to be deported from Vienna. We did not know where we would be deported to. But we were made aware every day that we would not survive in Vienna. I too was constantly afraid of being evacuated.' Such fears were entirely justified. Of the original 1000 'full Jews' left in Vienna in early 1943, only 198 were left alive by the end of the war.

Chapter 12

Vienna; Melbourne
1945 to 1947

The war in Europe ended in May 1945; Vienna had been liberated by the Red Army in mid-April.

The last few months of the war in Vienna were hellish. The bombardment of the city by Allied forces was ferocious; the small number of Jews who were still alive were required to sit in the levels of air-raid shelters most vulnerable to the bombing; many were killed; the violence of the SS against the few remaining Jews in hiding in Vienna, suddenly betrayed by neighbours and household spies in the dying days of the war, was systematic and brutal. Paula's chances of survival were small, as Paul clearly realised. He would wait for 'definite proof' of what he feared. For three months he heard nothing. Then in July 1945, Walter heard a report from Vienna dating from December 1944, nearly two years since the last sign of life. 'That is seven month[s] ago … Just waiting, that is all I can do,' responded Paul, who continued to use English for his correspondence, although the censorship of internment was no longer an issue. 'From my part there is nothing to report. I just keep going.' By 15 July, there was still no news: 'I really have nothing to report. Just as you say ... waiting is my pastime.'

But when he got home from work on 19 July, a telegram from Walter was waiting for him: it seemed that Paula might be alive.

> *Since six years the first bit of a lichtblick [ray of hope]. When I came home from work on Thursday the 19th I found your wire on my table. I immediately answered by cable: 'Thanks for cable is there possibility to communicate with Paula Red Cross can not help stop need her address.' Through our Red Cross one can still only send those Red Cross messages to Vienna. I wonder whether they ever reach the addressee. Have you over there other possibilities if so then send them my love please. Last week I also had your letter of June 4th. If this mail business only would improve a bit. Such a letter takes an awful long time. I am all right that means much better than I was one week ago.*

But a letter from Walter written one day after he had sent the cable seemed to extinguish any hope of a miracle: 'Two days ago I received your air mail letter of July 20th. Then things are not as bright as I saw them when I received your wire. In short "There is something fishy in the state of Denmark". And I still do not like this business over there. Wait and see, that is all I can do.'

A few days later, on 9 August, after three and a half agonising months of waiting since the liberation of Vienna, news finally came from Olga: Paula and her mother had survived. Paul's mother and other relatives had not.

> *May God bless you. I have your second air mail letter of July 26th. Sorry there is no air mail service from here to U.S.A. otherwise I would*

> *post by air mail. I had an air mail letter from Olga of the same date as yours in which she informed me that Rudolf (my uncle in Cardiff) had a letter from a lady in Prague saying that Tonie, Paula, Hans and Lisl are all-right. The lady got this information on June 15th. But all my other relatives are gone except two cousins.*

There was still no news about Martha Müller: 'The other day I had a letter from Dr. Martha Müller's mother, Irma Müller who lives in Sydney. She has not heard from Martha yet. It was hard for me to answer her letter. I myself would very much like to know about Martha.' There was no possibility of direct correspondence with Vienna – there was no mail service, the Red Cross offered only very limited forms of communication, and mail from elsewhere was slow. Paul's patience was exhausted, despite the good news. In mid-September, he wrote to Walter:

> *When I received your cable, so about two months ago I breathed a little bit after six years and then came again a black-out. It is a bit trying this waiting for direct news from our old country. You asked whether I have any plans for me and Paula. No I have none and I won't make any until I can get in direct touch with her and even then I won't make any plans. Look dear boy, I went through quite a different school during this last six years than you did and the result of my schooling was: not to plan anything anymore.*

Finally, in early October, he heard directly from Paula and from Tonie, letters written from Vienna on 1 September. In November, there was further communication from Paula.

I have two letters from my sister of Oct 20th in which she copies two letters from Paula, one of September 14th and one of Sept. 24th. Both were meant for my sister and for me. I do not think it is of any sense to write them to you as they mostly are concerned with very sad happenings, like my mother's death and Dr. Martha Müller's death.

Paul, in successive letters, repeated brief details of what he had learnt, all he could bear to share with Walter:

Herbert Schwarzwald in Brno [Moravio] is a genuine cousin of mine. His mother and my mother were sisters (née Willheim). He survived miraculously several concentration camps plus spotted typhus and was during the whole time and still is in contact with Paula. His mother perished unknown where during the occupation.

Herbert's mother was Mathilde's sister, Anna, who had lived with her in Theresienstadt and who had subsequently been murdered in Auschwitz.

Look, what would be the sense of telling you those stories or counting all those from my family who perished. Be sure they were quite a number and the method was a quite efficient one. I think that is sufficient information. As to Dr. Martha Müller, her story is too holy to be told. I wished I could humbly believe in heaven then I would be sure she being an angel now. By now I have written to her mother.

Paula had to break the news to Martha's brother, Paul, who had survived the war in Brussels: 'A couple of days ago Paul Müller from Brussels, the brother of Martha Müller, inquired at the IKG whether they knew my address. Hans got the card and I'll answer it today. He'll certainly want to know whether I can tell him anything about poor Martha. This case unfortunately is completely definite. Gas.'

During these months and into 1946, Paul attempted to get food parcels to Vienna via Olga, now working in a hospital in London, and via Walter. There were dire shortages there of all necessities, especially food and coal for heating; the winter of 1945–46 was particularly brutal. In November 1945, Paul had received his permanent residency in Australia, and in February 1946 would become an Australian citizen: 'That means I soon can apply for bringing Paula here, provided she wants to.' Paula's responsibility for her mother was now a factor. And communication with Vienna was not possible; everything had to go via Olga or Walter, and mail services from Australia to the US were hopelessly unreliable: 'The mail business to the States can't be called business anymore. It is absolutely out of order. I have no mail from you since ages and I do not know whether you ever get any of mine.' By December 1945, a month had gone by with no news whatsoever from Paula. More sad news came: Paula's mother, Tonie, with whom she had survived the war in Vienna, died in January 1946. She was seventy-seven. Looking back a year later, Hans wrote from Vienna: 'It is a year since Mama's death and so I will go and visit her in the Sephardic section. About Mama's departure I still cannot be comforted. The thought that she was not allowed to enjoy some years of happiness and quiet without fear still oppresses me.' At the same time, Paula wrote: 'For myself these are still difficult days and weeks. Soon it will already be a year. I still can't yet bear it well. Sunday we will go to the cemetery.' At the end of the same year, Hans wrote again about his mother, offering a glimpse of the mutual support among the family members in Vienna during the war years: 'I can't tell you how much Mama is still missed by me daily. Every day I had something to discuss with her. The Hitler years brought and forced us so much together; I was at her place several times a day.'

Late in 1946, Olga returned to Vienna as she could practise as a paediatrician there, whereas she could not in London, because of the opposition to émigré doctors in the local profession. Paula moved in with her. Conditions in Vienna continued to be extremely difficult; the winter of 1946–47 was also bitterly cold, and without heating the apartments were freezing, although Olga managed to get an allocation of coal for her consulting room in her apartment, where she conducted her private practice. Parcels from Australia and the US helped, although they could take a long time to arrive: 'This week a 10-kilogram parcel came from Paul via Jerusalem-Stockholm,' Paula wrote in December 1946. 'That also was very nice. It was en route since the beginning of September.'

Eventually such parcels were supplemented by international charitable relief. Paula was now free to join Paul in Australia. But this was proving extremely difficult. There were few ships available for this very long journey, and transit stops required the obtaining of transit visas, which were difficult to get. Paula was feeling deeply the effects of the traumatic experiences of the war and was barely able to write to New York.

> *Writing is so difficult for me. I am so disappointed that things are still going so slowly with my emigration and one advised me in a friendly way of 12 to 18 months waiting time. I'd like so much to be with Paul by now. But I don't need to tell you that, you know that too.*

> *There's a vague possibility that in January the American community organization will have a ship to Australia and I can get a place.*

She occupied a kind of emotional no-man's-land while this endless waiting went on: 'There really isn't much to tell about my current life,' she wrote.

> *I've got several acquaintances (hardly genuine friends) who sometimes visit us, and friends come from England to see Olga, so almost always there's someone visiting us or we're visiting someone. I'm already not entirely here anymore, really only externally. Very very seldom do we go to the theatre or to a movie. I go to the office every day but usually only for a while. I'm going to look for people who I've heard are departure-ready for Australia, to learn how they've arranged it. But it turns out that so far no one has actually boarded a ship. A lot of people have already left here and are staying in camps in places like Marseille, and so on. But I'd really like to avoid that.*

Suddenly, a way for Paula to be reunited with Paul appeared, in a cable from Paul's uncle, Rudolf Willheim, whom Paul had visited in London when he first arrived there in 1939. Rudolf had spent the war in England. Paula wrote:

> *Yesterday evening I received the following telegram from Rudolf: 'Ship places year waiting time air tickets soon obtainable stop. Pay the difference in travel costs. Wire whether February is convenient. Happy New Year.' I've now telegraphed the entire text to Paul and asked him to announce his opinion by telegraph. I'll get Paul's answer the day after tomorrow. You can imagine how anxious I am. Then I'll immediately*

have to begin to pack my tent. You can only bring a little luggage on the plane, but that's not so important. I can just have it sent after me a little later. It would be wonderful to be able to be with Paul so soon.

This generous gesture suddenly made travel possible. Not that the arrangements fell immediately into place: there were difficulties getting a transit visa for the United Kingdom, and if Paula used the opportunity to visit Walter and Lilly in New York, as she wished, this might involve a flight to New York and then overland to San Francisco, followed by plane or boat from there to Sydney. Separating from Hans was difficult: 'At Christmas Olga and I visited Hans and Lisl. It was very cosy and we enjoyed being with them. I'm always conscious on such occasions that it's the last time and that spoils it somewhat for me.' And she could hardly imagine her life in Australia.

I believe I could not learn the simplest things now or take a test. I have a brain like a sieve. I'm curious what will become of me in Australia. Whether my mental state recovers a bit. If not, I feel sorry for Paul. I just need to hear something about bookkeeping or some sort of commercial work and my hair stands on end. The idea of washing dishes, dusting, etc., to fill the days hardly appeals. And as a nurse there, they won't have time for an old thing like me. Besides I really don't have any proper education. So: we'll see.

Finally, it was all arranged, and Paula would fly the entire way, via New York. She left Vienna for New York on 12 March 1947, spent about a week there with Walter and Lilly, then flew on to San Francisco, where a close friend from Vienna now lived. Across the

Pacific there were stops in Honolulu and Nadi in Fiji; cables to Walter accompanied each stop on the route. Finally, on 25 March 1947, a cable arrived from Sydney: 'Paula arrived alright love Paula Paul.' It had been eight years.

Paul and Paula, July 1947

Chapter 13

Coda

Paul and Paula spent nearly twenty years together in Melbourne. Their first home was a small flat in a late 1930s block close to the centre of the city, where Paul was living when Paula arrived. It had a tiny bedroom and an uncomfortable bed ('here we have miserable beds like a stone'), but it did have a sitting room with some attractive art-deco features. There was a chronic housing shortage in Melbourne in the immediate postwar period as the servicemen returned and started families; they were given preference.

Shortly after Paula's arrival, news came that Paul's uncle Rudolf, whose generous assistance had allowed her to fly to be reunited with Paul, had suddenly died. 'Paul is very shaken by Rudolf's death. Now Grete is the last of this numerous family.' (Grete was the relative they had shared the flat with in Vienna after their marriage and until shortly before Paul's departure for England.) Socially, apart from his boss, Paul's most important contacts were those whom he had mentored in internment: 'Often in the evening his children come to him. They are young, dear young men who were interned with him. A lot of his former camp-comrades come.'

Where they would finally settle was unclear. Shortly after her arrival, Paula wrote: 'I have absolutely no homesickness for Vienna. Olga and Hans miss me. That is all.' An offer of work in the UK came, and with it the possibility of being closer to them, but, she wrote:

> *It is still too early to break off here. Paul is satisfied with his work and salary. The circumstances in Europe are still quite uncertain. Perhaps one will, or I will, be able to have a better overview of our situation in six months. In principle Paul and I have nothing against it, we're only in favour of going to Europe later. It's closer to everyone there. For that reason, I'm reluctant to have all the furniture and things sent here that Olga has kept for me.*

Paul had the idea of purchasing a house on a mortgage instead of paying rent, a very common practice in Australia at that time, which meant again that Paula needed to consider their future plans:

> *Paul is thinking over whether he should buy a little house. No, he hasn't won the jackpot! It's often done like that here. You pay a couple of hundred pounds on account and the remainder weekly in an amount that is a little higher than the rent we are paying (4 pounds, weekly, for example) for our rather inadequate apartment. Strangely I have, in fact, absolutely no opinion about this. I don't think that we're going to remain here forever, and we have no children. But in a few years the little house would be completely paid off, and in the meantime the rent being paid would not be thrown away but capitalized. We'll see.*

The anniversaries in January of the death of her sister and her mother, and other family dates, drew her thoughts back to Vienna:

'On December 11th our parents would have had their 60th wedding anniversary. And on the 13th it would have been Grandmama's birthday. And then come all the terribly sad January remembrance days. I often have a terrible longing to go to their grave.'

But in the end, they did stay, making regular trips to Europe and America to see Olga and Walter; Hans, an inveterate smoker, had died only fifteen months after Paula's arrival in Australia. He was not yet sixty. Several years later in 1953, Paul's modernist house, a reminder of Vienna, was built. The garden was planted with Australian native trees and plants, a shock to the neighbours, who preferred strictly European gardens. They enjoyed the house, and Olga came to visit.

Paula, Paul and Olga at Sunburst Ave, July 1956

They got on well with the neighbours, though Paula found the social rituals odd:

Because our suburb is like a small English provincial city, we have been invited by most of the surrounding neighbours and have also invited them to our place. At these get-togethers one talked about garden, garden, garden and weather, and according to the English manners the conversation never takes the least personal turn. Though we were not brought up to be effusive and loquacious, in the end I'm still always puzzled by this kind of 'party', how on earth these people manage to avoid in conversation everything which could halfway interest (me!).

Lessons learnt in Vienna had stayed with Paul: 'My neighbours are all nice,' he said years later, 'but I know they could turn on me at a moment's notice.'

He and Paula took trips to Tasmania, to Sydney, which Paula loved, and to Europe and New York.

In February 1966, Paula died, of longstanding heart disease. She was sixty-nine. Paul was inconsolable. He decided that he should spend time with Olga in Vienna: 'It is an old story but stays eternally new, and to whom it occurs it breaks the heart in two. I have my sister in Vienna, lonely. Whether I like Vienna or not does not count. For the time being everything is blurred, foggy, no hope of rational thinking. But I feel I should live with my sister wherever it is.'

In May, he made it to Vienna:

Here I am in Vienna with my sister. I arrived here on the 19th completely knocked out. Flying is no pleasure anymore. Packed like sardines. Lilly I do not think I will be able to go back via New York. I am too exhausted just a wreck. Things do not get easier. I have to be back at work by middle of July. Lilly I thank you very much for your invitation. Maybe one day I will turn up.

Coda

In June, he wrote to Walter:

I have not had a letter from you since a long time. Not that I can write anything, life just drifts on. I am staying here with Olga and later in this month we will be going to Yugoslavia for a fortnight and in July I will be going back to Melbourne. It sounds all so easy and so simple, doesn't it. Like hell it does. Write again one day. Ever done any thinking to find out what's important and what's totally unimportant? Just try it. You'll be amazed to find how very very very little really matters, really is important – and that little bit is important. No philosophy behind it.

After the visit to Yugoslavia, he wrote again to Lilly:

We came back from Yugoslavia just one week ago. It was quite nice. Strange and forgotten. A different world altogether. Time has stood still there for decades. Lilly I really thank you for your kind invitation. But I can't. I'm still not fit for human consumption. It wouldn't work. It doesn't work here either. I go back to Melbourne on the 23rd and will try to bury myself in work, hard work. Maybe it will work. Maybe not. Time doesn't help and Vienna didn't help. Please do write again one day to Melbourne.

When he returned to Melbourne, things were still not easy and stayed that way until the end of the year. 'Not much to write about me. I'm working, reading, writing. People write to me from Vienna and I answer. At the factory they're pathetically kind and nice to me, the toughest rogue there treats me like a kitten. Time does nothing but makes me used to ...'

A year after Paula's death, Paul flew again to Vienna to be with Olga, and this time he visited New York en route. He warned Walter and Lilly: 'I would like to let you know ahead of time, when you see me pull yourself together, don't get a shock. I have shrunk considerably especially my skull ... And please just be casual (that applies especially to Walter) or I'll collapse. The stronger sex is not worth a cracker.' The visit, however, seemed to mark some turning point. When he arrived in Vienna, he wrote to Walter, thanking him:

> *I was happy at your place and I felt at ease with all of you and I somehow felt that you all were not unhappy to have me there. It is not much I can write, the emotions still have too much hold of me. I'll just report: The flight to London was uneventful. Plenty of space. We arrived in London on schedule. Bus ride and taxi through my beloved London to Paddington Station. Cardiff: Grete & husband & Olga at the station. Two nights at Grete's house with love and warmth for a lost relative. I met all the people I wanted to meet there. Yesterday back to Vienna with Olga, and here I am sitting now writing to you, to Melbourne, to Cardiff. What a life. Another 18 days and I'm again on the move. I don't promise anything. I only hope to see you all again in not too far away a time.*

A year later, on another visit to Olga, Paul wrote about the impossibility of joining her permanently: 'It is a lovely country, even more than that, and still one cannot live here anymore.'

Paul lived for ten years after Paula's death; for three years from 1968, he had the company of his New York niece, Pat ('Penny'), and her friends, one of whom stayed on living at Paul's house for a year or two after Pat's return to the United States. In September 1976, when he was about to turn seventy-five, he wrote:

Coda

I am laid off, ill. The medicos do treat me to their best abilities. So no Vienna this year. Many thanks for your letter, specially about the times concerning your children. Main thing all of you are all right. A short time ago I had a letter from Penny which I already answered & told her about my illness, that is as much as I know about it. Tests are being made & treatment tried & that is all. I'll let you know once definite results can be obtained. Spring is slowly trying to wedge in, into a miserable winter.

Paul died the following month. Olga wrote to Walter:

I don't know whether someone from Melbourne has let you know that Paul died on October 22. He had liver cancer and was not sick for very long. The last weeks he was in a hospital where one did not let him suffer, his doctor was a friend – if there is any consolation for me, it is just this, that he did not suffer and fell asleep peacefully. Throughout it he did not want me to go there.

Paula had been buried in Vienna, with Martin, Tonie, Alice and Hans. Paul was buried alone in Melbourne. And so, their story ended. But in these pages, it lives on.

Postscript, 2021

Working on the story of Paul and Paula has, at times, had an uncanny quality, as if there were some guiding hand. In 2019, I wondered whether the flat where Paul and Paula had been reunited still stood. Pat thought not; she had once checked out the address, 11/135 Grey Street, East Melbourne, on a visit to Melbourne, when the block of flats there had not seemed to her old enough to date from Paul's time. I realised that it was in the same street as the oncologist I was seeing, and on my next appointment I checked out the building, which turned out to be right next to my oncologist's rooms.

The block was called Hayling and had obviously once been the site of one of the grand Victorian houses that filled the rest of the block. It occurred to me that this might be Paul's building, as it had a slightly art-deco look that seemed to me to predate the 1950s. The letterboxes in the entrance were also all large wooden boxes, unlike the streamlined metal ones of more recent design. When I got home, I researched online. Hayling, 135 Grey Street – there was a history: yes, there had been a beautiful Victorian house there, which had been pulled down and replaced by the flats in the late 1930s.

So, it was the one. I decided I would write to the current occupant of Flat 11 and see if they might let me in to look at it. As I scrolled down the page, I came across real estate advertisements. And suddenly, there it was: 'Open for Inspection, Flat 11, 135 Grey St,

East Melbourne'. It was for rent, and available for inspection the following morning.

There were only a few of us interested in seeing the flat, my reasons having nothing to do with rental. The agent took us up the stairs; the flat was currently unoccupied. It was more or less untouched since the 1940s, certainly in terms of layout, though the kitchen and bathroom had obviously been modernised. It was deeply moving to see the layout, the style of the place, the size of the tiny bedroom, the rather attractive art-deco touches in the hall, the living room, the door frames and windows, the decorative fireplace, the view from the window. I explained to the agent why I was there, and how much it meant to me to see it, and she generously let me stay on after the others had gone. There was 'no hurry'; she was struck by the story, and the coincidence.

I wrote to Pat that night about the extraordinary discovery and the sudden opportunity to see the flat, and what I had discovered there. She responded by pointing out that in the letter that Paula had written to Walter on her arrival in Melbourne, she had described the flat in detail and accompanied it with a drawing, which corresponded exactly to the current layout:

Our apartment is small but nice and looks more or less like this ...

Toilet and bath
Small bedroom (like your closet)
Living room (somewhat bigger than yours)
Kitchen (with many drawers and racks and sink and table and 2 chairs)
Front room (like yours only still narrower).

Postscript, 2021

Everything is very light and friendly and furnished. The furniture is definitely not to my taste. But for the moment we can't do anything about that. The kitchen furnishings, especially the kitchen dishes and cooking things, are as good as nothing. Not a single cooking spoon, strainer, nothing, nothing. Nothing. I'll have to assemble the necessities slowly. Everything outrageously expensive. For the moment I can't cook anything because I have no cooking things. So we eat quickly: ham, speck, eggs, butter, crackers, fruit, jam, and potatoes and salad and fish. Poor devil, eh?

I had felt Paul's and Paula's presence in the flat. I got a sense of the renewed intimacy, expressed in Paula's letter, after so many years of separation and suffering. I felt witness to how their life had resumed there. But it was part of a longer project of witnessing – this book, dedicated to them.

Paula and Paul at home in Melbourne, 1959

Acknowledgements

My introduction to the Jewish world of Holocaust survivors in Melbourne came through Lillian, who was a fellow literature student and became my soulmate, a relationship that has lasted for over fifty years. Lillian is an only child and each of her parents is the sole survivor of their family. Through my adult years, she gave her support lovingly and unstintingly, and had a profound effect on my life.

I want to say thank you to my friend Isaac, who has been a strong and caring support, particularly in the recent years of my illness. And he arranged an SBS radio interview about Paul and Paula.

This book has been made possible through the friendship of several others. Paul's niece, Pat Haim, introduced me to Paul when Pat and I were studying second-year English literature together at Melbourne University. Paula had died two years earlier and Pat spent a year supporting Paul on her transfer from New York, which she extended for the duration of her degree. This was the beginning of friendships among a group of literature students that lasted several years. Paul was fond of Pat's student friends; he made weekend meals for us, talked to us and educated us about the past – we discussed history, politics and life in general. A close friendship developed between Paul and me, and Pat has remained a friend through all the years since. In particular, she shared with me the surviving correspondence between her father

Acknowledgements

and his family, which she translated after his death. These form the basis of Part 2 of this book.

Peter Banki has been central to preparing the manuscript for publication. He stepped in while I was struggling with the task. I also owe a debt of gratitude to Julia Carlomagno and Kate Morgan from Monash University Publishing, who have been unfailingly encouraging and offered practical help. My Vienna friends Brigitta and Thomas Busch have also been a great source of support throughout.

About the Author

Tim McNamara (1949–2023) was a Redmond Barry Distinguished Professor Emeritus at the University of Melbourne. During his internationally successful career in applied linguistics, he established the Melbourne Graduate Program in Applied Linguistics (in 1987) and the Language Testing Research Centre (in 1990). In 2021, he was made a Member of the Order of Australia for his significant service. His work on language and identity over the course of his esteemed career culminated in his landmark book *Language and Subjectivity* (2019).